THE
REVOLUTIONARY
Who's Raising You

Empowered Parenting and Spiritual Psychology

DEIDRE STEADMAN

BALBOA.
PRESS

A DIVISION OF HAY HOUSE

Balboa Press books may be ordered through booksellers or by contacting:

Balboa Press
A Division of Hay House
1663 Liberty Drive
Bloomington, IN 47403
www.balboapress.com.au
1 (877) 407-4847

Because of the dynamic nature of the Internet, any web addresses or links contained in this book may have changed since publication and may no longer be valid. The views expressed in this work are solely those of the author and do not necessarily reflect the views of the publisher, and the publisher hereby disclaims any responsibility for them.

The author of this book does not dispense medical advice or prescribe the use of any technique as a form of treatment for physical, emotional, or medical problems without the advice of a physician, either directly or indirectly. The intent of the author is only to offer information of a general nature to help you in your quest for emotional and spiritual well-being. In the event you use any of the information in this book for yourself, which is your constitutional right, the author and the publisher assume no responsibility for your actions.

Any people depicted in stock imagery provided by Thinkstock are models, and such images are being used for illustrative purposes only.
Certain stock imagery © Thinkstock.

Print information available on the last page.

ISBN: 978-1-5043-0446-7 (sc)
ISBN: 978-1-5043-0447-4 (e)

Balboa Press rev. date: 10/06/2016

CONTENTS

DEDICATION

This book is dedicated to my beloved parents, Ruth and Chris. Mum always provided me with an exquisite example of the Divine Feminine. She laid the foundations for my own intuition, my patience, and my compassion. She is my wisdom. Dad always provided me with a powerful example of the Sacred Masculine. He laid the foundations for my own confidence, my clarity, and my boldness. He is my strength.

PREFACE

I have always wanted four children! Unfortunately my ten-year marriage was a tumultuous one, but I can't deny that it was a gold mine for my spiritual enlightenment and psychological empowerment. Throughout my ten years of marriage, I would don my hard hat and tote my pickaxe as I went in search of the psychological gems of relationships, marriage, family, parenting, and children. I would spend hours mining for the spiritual and psychological truths embedded there. My work as a clinical psychologist perfectly augmented this quest.

For a decade, I've spoken with parents, couples, children, and adolescents in a professional capacity. I have emerged from these psychological tunnels with grime on my face and aching muscles, but I found what I was searching for. I have acquired clarity and insight into the nuances of the mind. Not only that, I have discovered the intricate and sublime inner workings of relationships.

I am utterly fascinated by the psychology of individuals, particularly children. What's more, I am ravenous about the convergence of *me* and *you*. This intersection point is the stuff of *we*, of *us*. As I sat with client after client, delving deep into the psychological milieu of their marriage or their parenting, I was regularly awestruck by the perfection of every single rendezvous. As I spoke to clients in a professional setting about empowerment, I was refining and reinforcing it for myself personally. As I spoke about assertiveness and authenticity and wisdom to my clients, I was cementing them for myself personally. As I spoke about love and acceptance and compassion to my clients, I was fortifying it for myself personally...although I wasn't aware of it at the time. My clients became my angels. As Ram Dass would say, I was "polishing my mirror," and as I taught so did I learn. Psychology has been my vehicle for empowerment and enlightenment. But…I did always want four children….

I have three wonderful, gorgeous children ages eight, six, and four. They bring me endless joy, and they frequently teach me wonderful, welcome lessons. But towards the end of my marriage I felt an ineffable pang for another child. I would write it off as trying to fill a void and rebuke myself for such an ignoble thought. Then one day, I felt inspired. I saw the light. I had the ah-ha moment. It wasn't exactly an angel at the foot of my bed, but to me it was just as good. I received a knowing that my child would be called Grace.

Don't misunderstand—I do not have four children. I do not have a literal fourth child called Grace. This is not one of those stories. I believe that my revelation was a portent for the work you currently hold in your hand. You see, my work as a clinical psychologist has answered my prayer. Sappy? Yes! But true. It is intoxicating to me to sit and fellowship with my clients. My work is my offering, and during a consultation with clients, I sit mindfully allowing, as much as possible, a namaste moment to unfurl. This book is the culmination of ten years of prayerful communion with countless children and teenagers and parents and couples. But don't tell my clients that—they thought they were just coming to see a "regular" psychologist, not some crackpot who's tryin' to love them and stuff.

While clients thought they were coming to my office to learn about the practicalities of parenting and the logistics of their child's psychology, they were actually entering a temple of my own making. In the same way, I would like to lay this book upon the altar in your mind. I would like to offer you a little bit of my beloved Grace. You see, my work is Grace. My vocation has been grace-filled for me personally, and it is my hope that this work is a little bit of grace for you also. I have been blessed to discover personal empowerment and spiritual enlightenment within the hallowed halls of psychology. It is my sincere desire that you might you find some empowerment as a parent within these grace-filled pages too.

ACKNOWLEDGEMENTS

I would like to express my appreciation for, and deepest gratitude to, the spiritual teachers and thought leaders who have, unbeknownst to them, walked beside me along my path of empowerment and enlightenment. They have each held my hand and taken me, to greater and lesser extents, over and under and around and through this journey we call life: Esther Hicks (and the non-physical consciousness known as Abraham), Jane Roberts (and the non-physical consciousness known as Seth), Dr. Helen Schucman (who "scribed" *A Course in Miracles*), Dr. Brene Brown, Eckhart Tolle, Marianne Williamson, Caroline Myss, Rob Bell, Anthony Robbins, Iyanla Vanzant, and Oprah Winfrey.

ACKNOWLEDGMENTS

INTRODUCTION

I believe that spirituality and psychology make perfect bedfellows. Throughout our history, we have been captivated by the human condition. Psychology, at its best, is the study of the human psyche—the human mind. Throughout our history, we have been equally transfixed by the human spirit. Religion, at its best, enhances our understanding of the human soul.

In my opinion, empowerment and enlightenment are almost synonymous. The union of spirituality and psychology is a marriage made in heaven, and I would like to apply that to one of our most challenging but rewarding pursuits: parenting. Usually, when a parent is linking in with a psychologist about their child, it's not because their child is too "good" or too amenable. Most often, it is because their child seems angry or oppositional or depressed or anxious or merely won't pay attention or focus. Very frequently, it has been a doctor or an educator who has suggested that a psychologist might be helpful.

Now, at the risk of putting you off from the very beginning, I'm about to express something quite controversial. Doctors or educators or other parents or ministers or grandparents or even some psychologists don't necessarily have any expertise on *your* child. In fact, in my experience, often two parents don't agree between themselves regarding their own child, let alone a stranger having some specially acquired knowledge (says the psychologist—yes, the irony isn't lost on me). Why do I say this right off the bat? I want to see if I can change your mind about your exceptional child.

I sincerely hope that this book brings you some empowerment and enlightenment regarding your marvellous tween or your amazing teen or your rambunctious toddler. In order to change some of your beliefs—potentially strong and long-held—about parenting and emotions and diagnoses, I may need to dismantle some preconceptions. I may need to take a proverbial wrecking ball to the house of cards our society has built regarding the psychology and psychopathology of kids.

Within these pages, you will come to clearly see that I am a lover of the fiercely independent, and I know that I am probably among the few. As a psychologist, I have very unconventional but psychologically accurate opinions about kids, tweens, and teenagers who are considered problematic. I am one of the rare professionals who scoff at diagnostics like ADHD (attention deficit hyperactivity disorder) and ODD (oppositional defiant disorder). I am extremely reluctant to give merit to these kinds of terms, and I absolutely refuse to use such terminology myself.

The reason I bring a radically different psychological perspective to challenging kids is because I powerfully understand the human psyche. I am an advocate for a new psychology—awakened psychology. Old psychology and traditional parenting are fast becoming obsolete, and we are stretching into a new age. At the basis of this new understanding is the fact that fierce independence is an asset, *not* a liability.

I would suggest to you that we are in the throes of a global reawakening, and spiritual truth is permeating mass consciousness to a degree that it hasn't done before. The bedrock of society is shifting, and spiritual principles are coming to the fore. At the basis of spiritual psychology is, needless to say, spirit.

To elaborate, traditional psychology has regarded human nature essentially as a triad: the convergence of thought, emotion, and physicality (or action). Spiritual psychology regards the human experience as a tetrad of spirit, emotion, thought, and physical nature. In seeking to understand the human gestalt, it is my opinion that this spiritual lens is the most crucial. When we overlay our understanding of children with a spiritual understanding, I believe we bring both into sharper focus. It is my staunch belief that character traits deemed negative by prior generations are more a reflection of the social norms and directives of the time than indicative of sound psychological principles, much less spiritual truths.

I'm sure your upbringing was similar to mine. I was raised by very loving but traditional parents. Growing up, I was inclined towards conformity; my personality was sensitive, introverted and kind-hearted. I wanted to please others very much, and I was intuitive enough to know what pleased and what displeased. Put simply, I was extremely masterful at playing the good girl. I was a good chameleon. I could sense what somebody wanted to hear, I could sense how somebody wanted me to be or behave—I could always just sense it. I was absolutely not the squeaky wheel.

My intuitive, sensitive, kind nature was a great asset for me growing up. I pleased friends, I pleased teachers, and I pleased my parents. Traditional parenting aligned very well with my personality, because I was intrinsically motivated to be good. It suited me to be good. I had no trouble with it, and I was praised for it. Fortunately for me, my personality traits naturally fell into this socially constructed category of "good."

When I look back now on my nature as a young girl, there are distinct qualities that, while they contributed to my good-ness, did not serve my empowerment. On the one hand, other people were pleased with me and regarded me positively. In fact, other people often overlooked me because I wasn't a problem. On the other hand, I lacked confidence in myself. I was shy and often found attention uncomfortable. I lacked healthy self-esteem and questioned my own opinions a lot. I was much more likely to follow than to lead. I was not equipped to assert myself well, and I would easily sacrifice my own desires or preferences for others. When they were handing out the psychological assets of the rebel, I must have been standing in the queue for the bathroom.

A random example of my conformist nature that comes to mind took place when I was about seven or eight years old. I grew up with three siblings. My father worked for the public railway system while my mother stayed at home to raise us. We never had a great deal of money, and hard work and responsibility were instilled early. I had saved up my money to buy a book at the local bookstore in my small town. I still remember the exhilaration and pride I felt walking into a quaint little country bookshop with my "own" money.

I had my eye on a copy of Roald Dahl's *The BFG* (still a classic in my opinion). The book was just perfect, and I loved the feel of it in my hands as I cradled it to the counter—the crisp corners and glossy cover. When I got the book outside and eased it open, being careful not to crack the spine, I noticed that it had been assembled wrongly; some pages weren't ordered correctly, and some pages were missing entirely. I'm sure you can guess what an unconfident, self-sacrificing, shy little girl does when she experiences the disappointment and disheartenment of a faulty product. She does nothing!

Until now, I have never told anybody about that lovely book that was all wrong inside. In many ways, I think it's a very apt metaphor for myself as a young girl. I was nice, I was good, for all intents and purposes I was a perfectly behaved child, but inside I was insecure. I learned how to avoid discipline, but I forgot how to feel empowered. I could easily do as I was told, but I lost my own voice. I avoided making a fuss and never learnt how to *make* a fuss, even when it became necessary.

I intimately understand the trade-off that conformity demands because I, along with many others, struck the bargain. Other people were pleased, but often I was not. It is like doing a deal with the devil, and the devil is our social conditioning. The devil is our prioritisation of conformity over happiness, following the flock over forging your own trail.

Just for the record, I harbour no ill will towards my parents; they were merely a product of their own upbringing. They followed the parenting norms of their day just like their parents before them, and their parents before them and their parents before them. I understand why, culturally, "being good" has been a huge asset, but I also appreciate how sometimes it is just as much a liability.

Our history as human beings has not been without struggle, and our ancestors often lived hard lives. It was taken for granted that children didn't have the luxury of an easy childhood; there were wars, depression, poverty, and diseases to deal with. Conformity allowed society to function more smoothly and predictably.

As a result, we began to lump children into two gross piles: "good" and "bad." But the tacit meaning was "conformist" and "rebellious." To put it another way, you were deemed good if you did what you were told, and you were considered bad if you did not do what you were told.... it's not romantic, it's not inspiring, it's not empowered, but it's simple.

As an adult, with my years of psychological training and my own psychological mastery, I have come to realise that my rebellious nature was never bad. It just represented more assets— untapped assets, wild assets. As society assigns human behaviour to gross categories of good and bad, right and wrong, healthy and unhealthy, we end up living in a black-and-white dichotomy. It is my opinion that this is a bastardisation of spiritual truth and serves no higher purpose within parenting, education, religion, or anything really.

I know that is putting it in very strong terms, but if we are to accept that human beings have a non-physical nature—a spiritual, divine nature—then any human behaviour should be scrutinised through this lens first and foremost. For me personally, I now utilise my nonconformist nature in ways that serve me exceptionally. I no longer consider any facet of my nature to be bad or wrong. I understand, however, that others may misinterpret or misconstrue my actions and label my opinions or actions in those terms.

Case in point: I am writing here about pioneering psychology and parenting into new frontiers. I am bucking traditional psychology and personally revelling in the dynamic, leading-edge nature of it all. I also appreciate that some may misunderstand my sentiments and strongly disagree, and that puts me in danger of attracting the label "wrong." But for myself, I have struck a perfect balance between my good and bad natures—better said, my tame and wild natures.

I am still as kind-hearted as ever. Indeed, I would say that with empowerment comes a greater capacity for love and kindness. But I also understand that it's not my job to please or rescue anybody. I have found compassion with a healthy dose of assertion. I have found kindness with a helping of confidence. So, when all is said and done, I'd like to take terms that leave a sour taste in my mouth—like oppositional, hyperactive, or defiant—and rework them so they reflect more of their spiritual essence.

We have done our children such a disservice by seeking to suppress their unique, individual, fierce, nonconformist natures in the name of good parenting. We are leading them astray by indoctrinating them into a culture that has strong leanings towards conformity. We are living at a time where depression and anxiety are at unprecedented levels, and we are literally forgetting how to be happy and peaceful. I would like to turn this all on its head and suggest that your wild children are actually the psychological masters among us.

Children, by and large, know how to better orient themselves to happiness and contentment than their adult counterparts. That is, until they reach a certain age; then they can be overly influenced by the prevailing cultural ideology. Nevertheless, traditional parenting presumes that adults know better. Think about that for a moment. What exactly do adults know better? Depression! Anxiety! Conformity! Rule-following! Social expectations! Stress!

Wild children refuse to sit in a box stamped "meek and mild." They are outlaws, rebels, revolutionaries, they are the pioneers. They are the ones who are revered by the following generations but sometimes are mocked within their own. Sound familiar? I am not exaggerating when I say that revolutionaries like Martin Luther King or Jesus or Gandhi are cut from the cloth of the rebel. Society will typically seek to criminalise nonconformity (hence my distaste for terms like ADHD or ODD, which can mean little more than "junior criminal"), but as parents, educators, and professionals, we can esteem all facets of human nature. After all, if it is true that we are all spirit first and foremost, then a namaste consciousness suggests that there is advantage to all aspects of our humanity, because they are inextricably linked to our divinity.

CHAPTER 1

Conformity Isn't All It's Cracked Up to Be

I was speaking to a mother and father regarding their young son. The parents were in conflict about their differing parenting styles—and, needless to say, this was adding tension to the marital relationship. These parents were a wonderful microcosm of the larger parenting macrocosm, a perfect representation of the broader attitudes that we hold regarding our children.

The father considered his young son to be defiant, and he felt that his son's behaviour was malicious and spiteful. "He just likes pushing my buttons," he'd remark. He thought his son was undisciplined and that he wouldn't succeed in life because he could not follow rules and did not respect authority. This father would often express himself with comments like:

"He just won't do as he's told."

"He just starts to run amok."

"He goes to whine to his mother because I won't let him do what he wants."

"I just can't get through to him."

The mother, on the other hand, sought to protect their son. In her opinion, the boy was a scapegoat who was being unfairly targeted. He was being picked on and therefore needed to be defended. While there was no question that these parents loved their son, their respective approaches were indicative of the psychological errors we make when parenting. The flawed premises we hold can sprout erroneous beliefs that then give birth to futile action.

Because it is reflective of a large portion of society, let's first take the father's mentality. His tactic with his son was a punitive, "pull yourself up by your bootstraps" approach. As the psychological underpinning of this approach is conformity, it is a stifling of individual freedom—and this was triggering a defiant, independence-seeking reaction in his son.

It is in our nature to sometimes cut off our nose to spite our face. When pushed, we will sometimes resist for resistance's sake. From an onlooker's perspective (and let's face it, there are plenty in the peanut gallery ready to level opinions about your parenting, even when they don't have children themselves), freedom-seeking behaviours play out as rebellion. They manifest as naughtiness in some opinions. However, at the heart of this type of behaviour is an assertion of individuality, authenticity, free thinking, and free choice. No human being likes to be dictated to. It triggers a fierce response. Why do you think wars happen?

Imagine you've started a new job and are enthusiastic about it. You know you can do the job well, and you have a talent for it. You know yourself to be hard-working and well-meaning. You also want to perform at your best for a company you believe in. All in all, your spirits are high, and you hold positive expectations.

However, what if you have a boss who criticises your work performance? Maybe it doesn't start out that way—perhaps your boss is diplomatic and polite about the critique when performance reviews come around—but nevertheless, it knocks your confidence somewhat. However, you still want to perform well, and you mostly like your boss. You rationalise the experience with thoughts like, *He's just trying to get the best out of me, I guess.*

Now imagine that the negative comments come more regularly and are more like thinly veiled judgements: "Not on the ball again today?" or "It's not really that hard to grasp, is it?" What if you are directly criticised: "You just can't get this right" or "How did you get this position?" or "I'm just waiting for an excuse to fire you!" What if this happens every day? If your boss's management style resembles bullying more than supervising, I guarantee you will end up hating this person (and your job). Anybody would. Anybody with a modicum of self-respect and independence would rebel. This approach would not get the best work performance from you; indeed, it would elicit the worst. You don't want to rise to your best when you anticipate criticism.

Criticism doesn't even need to be direct. Our instincts are well tuned; if you can even *sense* that a boss or co-worker doesn't especially like you, that's usually enough to dampen your enthusiasm. Let's face it: you're not about to go the extra mile for somebody who doesn't appreciate your effort or is downright antagonistic. It is psychologically healthy to assert yourself against suggestions that you are somehow "wrong" or "bad." To say it another way: it is psychologically healthy to get angry and defiant in this type of situation.

We teach kids to assert themselves in the schoolyard when they are being bullied, just as we encourage adults to assert themselves against management when there is discrimination or harassment. So why do we expect children to remain emotionally and psychologically buoyant when it's a parent offering subtle (but often painful) comments or judgements? Children are hardwired to love their parents; they are little emotional barometers. They can very quickly and accurately attune to a parent's disapproval or disappointment. You would absolutely hate going to a workplace where the emotional tone was one of disapproval or reproach, wouldn't you? But you don't love your boss as your children love you. Furthermore, you are an adult. Imagine the psychological impact upon a child who is subtly but clearly disapproved of.

Take the father we met earlier; he was sincere in his attempts to help his son but naïve about the psychological impact of his approach. He was expecting his son to be able to receive disapproval and negative judgement—from somebody he loved, no less—without having an anger response or a guilt response or feeling a sense of failure. Unfortunately, it is psychologically impossible for a child to sense recrimination yet remain psychologically buoyant, happy, focused, attentive, and optimistic.

These kids often find themselves in a double bind: "Dad wants me to perform at my best, remember and follow the rules, and make few mistakes. I desperately want to do this for him because I love him and I want his approval, but I somehow get it wrong, and the stress and pressure of being good paradoxically makes me more likely to be bad." The ultimate tragedy of this merry-go-round of pain is that it is most likely when kids are happy (laughing, playing, shouting, etc.) that their behaviour is considered disruptive to adults.

Think about it: When kids are happy, they are like puppies. They bounce off the walls, get noisy, are exuberant, and become effervescent, talkative, playful, and sometimes even snappy. Can you imagine the confusion for kids when they are literally feeling their best and yet are reprimanded for it? "Simmer down!" they are told. "Be quiet!" they are rebuked—just for acting as a happy child naturally acts. I have found myself uttering these words to my six-year-old son. These words almost gagged me as they came out, yet they came out nonetheless. Yes, I can espouse the benefits of nonconformity and still struggle with my own selfish desire for conformity. When I want to go to sleep and my son seems at his happiest (which is a polite way of saying he is boisterous and effervescent), it is something of an art to strike a balance between my wants and his wants. At times, I have wondered what would happen if I started jumping on the bed and face-diving into the pillows with him.

When children are guided away from their own happiness towards pleasing a parent, they learn how to please others but forget how to please themselves. This is a recipe for conformity. In the name of good parenting, we unwittingly elicit guilt, sadness, remorse, anger, or hopelessness from our kids while simultaneously guiding them away from spontaneity, happiness, playfulness, confidence, and the like. Conformity demands a trade-off: something needs to be psychologically sacrificed in order for human beings to conform.

To some degree, emotional authenticity becomes the sacrificial lamb. Free thinking and individuality are hogtied to the nearest pole, marched to the volcano's edge, and thrown in. We have been taught that conformity is required for a successful life. You were encouraged to get a respectable job, to be sensible and practical, to get good grades, get along with teachers, do the lessons as instructed. Social principles are imbued with a mandate to conform. Social order ostensibly depends upon individuals following the rules; otherwise, we're in danger of anarchy...or so we're told. Morality ostensibly depends upon individuals following the tribe mentality; otherwise, we are in danger of debauchery on every street corner.

But here's the rub: we are *all* freedom-seeking by nature. We *all* strive to express ourselves uniquely and authentically. When social mandates, based upon conformity, thwart individual expression and free thinking, people revolt (anger response) or they begin to feel hopeless (sadness response).

I was channel-surfing recently, and I came upon a brief snippet of a documentary about prison inmates. In the few minutes that I watched, they showed a young man facing away from his cell door, a towel over his head. He had stacked a chair on top of a table and was endeavouring to sit upon it. I assume it was his private protest against some perceived injustice.

The thing that I found psychologically fascinating wasn't his behaviour; to some extent, I can imagine the impulse to hide away— hence the towel upon his head—and protest being in a cage. I get that. I understand feeling powerless and wanting to take control, even of something so minute as putting a towel over your head and placing a chair upon a table. There was an empowered, personal statement being made: "So there!" he seemed to scream. "You might have stuck me in this cage, but you can't stop me putting this chair up here." It was the psychological equivalent of a toddler sticking out his tongue in protest.

What I found psychologically fascinating was everyone else's reaction. There must have been about ten individuals outside of this cell door, I don't know their respective roles, but I can guess there may have been a nurse, a prison officer, the camera crew obviously, and maybe a supervisor. Everybody seemed intent on this man "simmering down," and it made me think that we respond to nonconformity in adults in the same way we do with children. The onlookers were insistent on this offender taking the chair down and taking the towel from his head.

Now, don't misunderstand. I have worked in a correctional facility, and I understand why things are done this way. It's not a lack of clarity on my part. I would just like to inspire some contemplation and suggest that we could improve the way we react to an anger response. This cadre of bystanders might as well have been a school principal, a school counsellor, a class teacher, and a camera crew. Our societal reaction to nonconformity changes little from infancy to childhood to adolescence to adulthood. It's just that our time-out corner gets bars.

Don't you think that with incarceration rates at record levels, with suicide statistics ever-climbing, with the prescription of psycho-pharmaceuticals at record levels, perhaps we could revisit the paradigm? Traditional is traditional—it is the dogma that is familiar and the principles that are common—but does it serve humanity?

Now, I can only begin to imagine the chain of events that would lead someone to serious criminal behaviour and thereby imprisonment, but I know without a doubt that it does not happen in a vacuum. Let me give you a very small, completely trivial example to see if I can pique some reflection.

Recently I took my children to swim in the local river. My dad came along, and he reminded me about lifejackets for the kids. Actually, he did slightly more than remind me. He politely (he is English, after all) stated that *he* would put lifejackets on the kids if it were up to him. I was surprised by my reaction, because I was slightly defensive—only slightly, but nevertheless.

Now, I know how sensible lifejackets are. I know how practical they are. I know the reason for them. Yet my instinctive response was defensiveness. I know that is a ridiculously superficial, silly example, but I'm sure you have experienced exactly the same to a greater or lesser extent. We are hardwired to want to do life on our own terms. We want to drive on our own terms, we want to eat on our own terms, we want to do chores on our own terms. We want to follow our own inner guidance.

Can you imagine if, across your entire lifetime, you were treated antagonistically every time you followed your own guidance? I'm sure you know as well as I do that there is often a predictable trajectory for young, angry kids within our society. They are constantly disciplined within the school system through exclusion, detention, and/or expulsion. This naturally elicits shame or humiliation or self-loathing or condemnation. When anger is the best emotion to be found amid this crappy collection of options, then more trouble is stirred up and more and more condemnation or shame or disapproval is elicited, which prompts more and more trouble and more and more anger... and around and around it goes.

If I can get prickly when told about lifejackets—something so minor and banal—and you can become snappy when, for instance, your partner asks you to do something you really don't want to do or agree with something you don't agree with, do you see how even "criminal" is a social construct when you pare it right back? For a kid in a classroom who won't sit still and listen, even if the lesson is boring and feels irrelevant, *naughty* is often the most complex psychological notion we have concocted. If you were considered naughty and treated combatively by teachers, who in turn influence your parents to treat you belligerently, who influence your grandparents to treat you with hostility ... pretty soon you would seek refuge with peers. Which peers would you seek refuge with? The most loyal ones, of course, the ones who won't turn on you, the ones who'd die for you. Oh wait, that's a gang!

Yes, psychologically, that is the evolution, or perhaps devolution. It's not bad, it's not wrong, it makes perfect sense when you understand how the human psyche works. Can't you see that when the people you literally love most have formed a fixed, negative, perhaps subtle (but subtle doesn't mean better) opinion about who you are—and when the people who seem to hold the most power and influence have formed a fixed, negative opinion about who you are—eventually you just want to turn your back to the prison door, stick a towel over your head, and put a chair on top of a table.

Let's briefly return to our example to regard the father who was experiencing difficulty with his "defiant" son. The final irony came when he realised that he too was raised by a traditional father. His individual expression, his authenticity, was often squashed by demands to "do as you're told"—even when what you're told guides you away from your own happiness and confidence and from knowing your own mind. When I asked this father if he, himself, responded well to this parenting style, his answer was a resounding no. He had experienced his own rebellion exactly as his son was demonstrating now. However, instead of this revelation being the catalyst for transformation and evolution in his own parenting, he justified his embrace of the traditional with the old catch-cry, "It didn't do me any harm." Well, in my professional opinion, it has done some harm, it has done all of us some psychological harm.

Let me take you back to our fictitious example of working for a harsh and critical boss. Imagine that this boss suddenly recognises that the gradual decline in your work performance is due to his berating. I know, I know, your boss would need to be a spiritual and psychological master to achieve this epiphany, but just run with the example for the sake of the example. Imagine your boss has an awakening and realises that your irritated, sullen, withdrawn, angry presence at work is mostly because of his approach to you. Imagine what a profound difference it would make for a boss like this to say, "Hey, you know what, I've realised that it can't feel very good to be criticised by somebody you once respected. I've realised that you are probably doing the best you can under very difficult circumstances. It must seem to you like I'm not easy to please, and I'm probably not if I'm honest. I know that you are a good person and you are sincere in wanting to do a good job."

Now I know that this fairy-tale ending is what Hollywood movies are made of and not the stuff of real life, but I just want you to extend this metaphor in your own mind to a child and parent. Children love their parents. Let me say that again: children love their parents. Let me repeat that for emphasis: *children love their parents*. No child is defiant for the hell of it. No child is antagonistic for the chuckles. No child is aggressive because it's fun. The aggression you observe, the antagonism you observe, and the defiance you observe is psychological pain. It's the child's best, in-the-moment attempt at confidence and resilience. It is the direct result of being told, subtly or not, by a parent or educator or society that he or she is bad or wrong.

One of the final messages I delicately attempted to convey to this father before he disengaged from therapy was the hypocrisy of his parenting approach. While every step along the way he endeavoured to make his child conform to his wishes, he himself could not change his *own* behaviour. While he understood the merit in what I articulated, and he appreciated that what I expressed was psychologically sound, he would not change his mind about his son's naughtiness. In exactly the same way that he accused his son of having rigid and fixed opinions and ideas, this father could not yield his own ideas and opinions either. His son was bad or problematic, and that was that. To say it more accurately, he would not change his mind because he was backing his own opinion; he was sticking to his own mind.

This father held staunchly to his own opinion even when challenged by a professional, and he was extremely resistant when challenged to yield. This was exactly the same behaviour that his son was exhibiting. For the son, it was termed *defiance*; for the father, it was considered *right*. Parents who experience, and label, their children as oppositional must themselves have an oppositional nature. It is the very nature of opposition that there are two warring factions. A peacemaker makes peace while a warmonger makes war.

If it takes two to tango—and indeed it does—then I would ask parents or educators or doctors or indeed psychologists, how easy is it for *you* to change your mind? Can you relinquish an opinion that you hold to be true and right? Now I'm not talking about whether a child's reality is objective truth; it is indeed subjective truth, but that isn't the point. My point is that it's the child we expect to change, it's the child we expect to yield, and it's the child we expect to submit. This is disempowerment in the making.

As an adult, if you yield to a discriminatory boss at work, it literally makes you depressed. It can make you anxious and stressed and altogether miserable. To say it another way, it makes you feel disempowered. The alternative route—the route to empowerment, or at least the first stop on the journey back—is to become angry and fed-up. Anger will eventually make you leave, because you simply refuse to conform.

Now I'm not saying that we throw the baby out with the bathwater and allow children to raise themselves. There are certainly some handy things that we adults can impart to them. But I am suggesting that we need to look deeper and harder at narratives that do little more than criminalise children. Nobody exists in a vacuum, and nobody chooses anger or defiance without provocation. I believe societally we can evolve beyond antiquated notions like "children should be seen and not heard" or "spare the rod spoil the child." I also believe we can evolve to a point where we revere and respect children's innate wildness as much as their inherent tameness.

So let us now meander back to our mother and father and their dilemma with their son. If dad was a no-man—"No, don't be noisy. ... No, just do as you're told. ... No, don't say things like that. ... No, stop doing that. ... No, you can't do that. ... No, you shouldn't touch that"—then surely mum being a yes-woman represented the solution. Right? Wrong!

CHAPTER 2

Saying No Can Breed Disempowerment ... and So Can Saying Yes

One of the most intriguing aspects of human nature is our dualistic thinking. By and large, people think in a dualistic way, a dyadic way—in other words, we think in terms of either/or. You are either my friend or my enemy. You are either right or wrong. You are either good or bad. The implications for this thought process are quite profound.

You might have even encountered this dyadic tendency within yourself when reading through the first chapter of this book. While I spruik the benefits of parents *not* saying no, many would assume that I'm therefore advocating *for* saying yes. If you're against one thing, you must be for its opposite—this is the dualism that I am describing.

Whenever I spoke with the mother and father described in Chapter 1 about their interactions with their child, it was a delicate balancing act, because I was always in danger of appearing to be on somebody's side. When I endorsed one parent's perspective, the other parent felt denounced. Parents in general assume that if I encourage one response, I am firstly designating it to be right and secondly, by extension, deeming the other response to be wrong. This oversimplified naughty-and-nice dyad is how traditional parenting and traditional psychology have come to their current predicament.

Parents are confused about their parenting because, to some extent, we have moved away from strict traditional approaches like smacking but have encountered a different problem: our dyadic nature. It is almost like we are raising the very notion of parenting itself. We are bringing it up. Parenting styles are socially evolving and growing up through infancy and childhood. To my mind, our ideas about parenting are now smack bang in the middle of their adolescence. They are awkward, clumsy, sometimes smelly, and downright impossible to completely understand. They lack the nuance and sophistication characteristic of adulthood. One hopes that with maturity comes an understanding that things are not black and white. There is a vast grey area.

For example, when society came to something of a consensus about not smacking, many parents assumed that it meant no discipline at all. In the confusing aftermath, parents have been left struggling to redefine and rework the very notion of discipline itself, and with this backdrop the stage was set for the inevitable. Many parents came to embrace the yes simply because it wasn't the no. I think modern parents are looking for an evolved and enlightened approach to parenting. We are hungry for a new, empowered paradigm. I believe that many parents are awakening to the limitations of traditional parenting but are now searching for empowered, psychologically savvy and spiritually shrewd alternatives. I think you'll agree that these kinds of dilemmas are the hallmarks of teen-hood.

In their efforts to claim individuality and independence, teenagers often revolt against their parents. While in my opinion this is a very good thing psychologically, for many teens this is done on principle rather than birthed from a deeper wisdom. Teenagers have an innate drive to move things forward, to pioneer into new arenas. Inherent within this natural evolution is discomfort with the gap between the old and the new worlds, the chasm of undifferentiated rules and nebulous principles. It is the netherworld between childhood and adulthood. Under these conditions, a yes can represent little more than no's opposite. I would suggest that modern parents have found themselves deep within this psychological abyss regarding their parenting. We are standing at the side of the ravine, ready for the trek across, and we must decide what we want to pack for the new world and what is worth leaving behind.

So while it may seem like I am advocating to leave no behind, before we teeter our way across the ravine on the rickety footbridge, it may also seem that I'm advocating to leave yes behind too. "But," I hear you say, "how would I even parent without offering the guidance of a yes or a no?" Perhaps you've garnered the impression that I'm advocating to pack yes but discard no. Or maybe you think that I'm recommending the reverse. If you're confused and you've thrown your hands in the air, exasperated, then my work here is done.

In fact, I am not trying to offer a specific strategy or formula for parenting. This is not parent-by-numbers. That has always been the fatal flaw of traditional parenting and traditional education and traditional religion and traditional media and traditional … well, everything, really. Rather than allowing inspired, authentic, and individual action, we rely overmuch on rote and prescribed ideologies—that is, conformity. To a greater or lesser extent, we do what we've always done because it's what we've always done. What I'm trying to get you to think about is the fact that revolutionary, pioneering, evolved parenting will not be formulaic. It is literally our concept of the concepts that I would like us to deconstruct and assess. It's like meta parenting.

But let me not get ahead of myself. Let us return to our example of the couple and their young son. While we spent some time in the first chapter unpacking Dad's approach and deciding what aspects are old and tattered and worth shedding into the crevasse, it's now time to put the psychological magnifying glass over Mum's approach and see what we find. If we typified Dad's approach as restrictive, we can characterise Mum's approach as permissive.

These parents were not just experiencing difficulties with their son's behaviour, they were experiencing marital difficulties too because their parenting styles were so different. Over time, Dad had embedded himself more and more firmly in his no, while Mum would often counterattack and anchor herself more securely in her yes. Mum would lament to me that her husband picked on their son and jumped on him constantly for little things. Dad would bemoan that his wife would let their son get away with anything and would not establish any boundaries or expectations. Mum would insist that her husband's approach was making their son fretful and despondent. Dad would insist that his wife's approach was making their son undisciplined and disrespectful. It was a classic case of two people in their respective corners, and they'd come out swinging round after round after round.

So what are the merits of a yes approach to parenting? Is there psychological value in it? Let me first clarify what I mean by a yes approach. The reason this couple is the perfect representatives for modern parents is because their respective ideologies are symbolic of traditional parenting versus contemporary parenting. As we have discussed, Dad's approach was highly traditional and built on a foundation of conformity and authority and rules. Mum's approach was much more redolent of a contemporary approach, a yes mentality. The psychological flaw of the contemporary approach is that it is still built on a shoddy foundation.

Our psychological tendency to boil everything down to a simple dyad has resulted in a paradigm shift from one extreme to the other. We wanted to throw out the bathwater, and we lose the baby right along with it. Within a few generations, we've ostensibly gone from a parenting philosophy based on toughening kids up and not coddling them to a parenting philosophy based on protecting and coddling kids—from "Kids need to learn that life is tough" to "I want my kids to have it easier than I did," from "He's old enough to know better" to "He's just a little boy," from "He's malicious and needs to respect authority" to "He's innocent and can interact with authority however he likes." Do you see how, after a while, this mental tendency we have to reduce complex human interaction into simple binaries means that we reduce and reduce and reduce until we're left with a pot of burnt, pungent muck? Ultimately, it begins to beg a larger question: Is our little boy happy? Even with a yes parent, the answer may be no.

A child does not necessarily find personal empowerment more easily with a more permissive parenting style. Why? Because the belief system that underpins this style can have its origin in notions of weakness or vulnerability. Isn't it interesting that when you peel back the layers of the proverbial parenting onion, both a permissive and a restrictive parenting style come from the same fundamental premise. As with most dualistic notions, on the surface they may appear at odds, but when you pull back the layers they are more in harmony than discord.

A restrictive parent believes that a child is weak and vulnerable and needs to harden up, whereas a permissive parent can also believe that a child is weak and vulnerable and needs protecting, needs rescuing. A parent may unintentionally provoke a child's wild nature and typically it is a restrictive, authoritative parent who triggers this type of response in a child. The wild nature is not, in itself, psychologically problematic. The wild nature is confident, it is assertive, it is about organisation and problem-solving and leadership – it is largely thought based. But if there is a lack of balance, this nature can become very fierce and dominant indeed. Conversely, a parent may unwittingly over-nurture a child's tame nature. Typically it is the more permissive parent who triggers this type of response. Again, it is not a tame nature in itself that is psychologically troublesome, but rather a lack of balance. The tame nature is sensitive, it is intuitive and kind, it is about helping and humility – it is largely emotionally oriented. When unbalanced, this nature can become very submissive and lack confidence.

From a psychological perspective, both of the parents I worked with were right and both parents were wrong. Additionally, both parents, while simultaneously right and wrong, were also both wise and foolish, all at the same time. Both parents were wise in the sense that they sincerely loved their son and honestly believed that they were protecting his interests. However, both parents were foolish in the sense that they believed that their own marital discord was not making a significant contribution to the emotional concoction that was their son's psychology. They remained rigid in their respective mindsets and brought little self-reflection and personal responsibility to the situation. They were content to merely blame the other. Psychologically speaking, there were aspects to both sides of the argument that had merit and were entirely valid, but this fact was, to a degree, rendered irrelevant because they were both hampering the self-esteem and confidence and empowerment of their son. This fact will trump any parent's personal sense of rightness every time.

So, I hear you inquire, why exactly is it that a yes approach is not psychologically empowering? Let me quickly reiterate here, lest you fall into your mental dualism trap, that I am not advocating for a blanket approach to parenting. In exploring the merits and pitfalls of a particular parenting style, we begin to gain something of an overview and, out of this, meta parenting can be considered.

Meta parenting is like riding in a hot-air balloon. You are close enough to the ground to make out the basic structures, survey the landscape, and even wave down to the people below, but, nonetheless, you are still hovering above. Your perspective is bird's eye, not ground level. In order to transform and revolutionise parenting through the lens of a new psychology, we must assume this advantageous perspective. Otherwise, we are just wandering about on foot not able to see the wood for the trees.

Remember that an either/or thought process is faulty and outmoded and will not suit our new psychology. So, back to our permissive parenting style. One the one hand, it is true that less rule-bound parenting is an improvement on a traditional approach because, in theory, it allows for more collaboration, spontaneity, and flexibility. However, while the theory may be sound, in practice the fatal flaw is borne out every single time.

Let me give you an example to see if I can clarify what I mean by the fatal flaw. Let's take the dynamic between the parents themselves. Within almost every relationship, an unconscious dynamic is established in which one person assumes the more dominant role while the other unconsciously assumes the more submissive one. When both people largely hold up their end of this unspoken bargain, things typically go well. But if one person attempts to break the tacit contract, problems ensue. Within the marital relationship of our couple, the husband was often assuming the submissive role, at least with regards to his marital relationship. He believed that if he put up with his discomfort about the way his wife was parenting and tried to acquiesce to her wishes, he was doing her a kindness. In being a yes-man, he was ostensibly being nice to her. His theory about kindness, though in line with pop psychology, did not hold psychological wisdom because his behaviour was built upon a foundation of self-sacrifice.

To say it another way, he was feeling disempowered but thinking himself to be helpful. His feelings and thoughts were out of sync. In thinking he was being kind to her, he was in actuality being unkind to himself. It's like that old saying about asking for one million dollars from the beggar on the street. You just can't give somebody something you do not possess, no matter how much you may wish to. Kindness cannot be born from disempowerment. Over time, resentment and bitterness were the natural result, because when you think you're being kind but you feel disempowered, that's not kindness—not self-kindness, anyway. It is bitterness masquerading as kindness, it is resentment dressed in drag.

When you set about trying to guess and predict how to aid in another person's happiness, you wind up serving two masters. You come up hard against this simple fact: you were not born to serve other people's happiness because you cannot truly fathom other people at their deepest. Even if you make an attempt to be their happiness, you soon realise that other people are too fickle. What makes them happy one day is different from what makes them happy another day. They are also too scattered and inconsistent for you to ever perform successfully. What they assume will make them happy one day does not actually make them happy, or even when you do as they request they seem unhappy with the way you have performed your task.

It is like being the king or queen sitting upon your own throne. Your kingdom is your own to rule as you see fit. While you may have advisors or knights acting as your wise counsel, ultimately you are the ruler, and your kingdom will stand or fall at your command. When you attempt to please another person from a psyche of lack or resentment or keeping score or keeping the peace, you are, in essence, stepping down from your own throne. You are usurped by somebody who does not know your dukes and knights intimately. You defer your own personal power to somebody who does not love your maidens and ladies as much as you do. You step down for somebody who does not know the nuanced principles of your governance. In seeking to be nice, in saying yes overly much, you end up vacating your throne in the hope that a new patriarch or monarch might do a better job for your subjects, but rather than King Arthur you end up with the Mad King.

You can never build the empowerment of another upon a foundation of self-disempowerment, no matter how nice you think it is. In case it has escaped your savvy eye, let me point out here the similarities between the son's natural psychological response to disempowerment and the dad's natural psychological response. Just as our father was working to keep Mum happy—and failing, and becoming resentful and disheartened and distant and angry—so too was the son working to keep Dad happy—and failing, and becoming resentful and disheartened and distant and angry. The psychological symmetry of it all is perfect.

As Dad, in his own mind, was being nice to his wife, the ultimate irony was that Mum did not appreciate his niceties. This is eventually and always the case within any relationship and it is why resentment dressed-up as niceness is the fatal flaw within many relationships. When somebody essentially abdicates the throne within his or her own mind, there is a deep psychological recognition on the part of the other. It either triggers the other to step into the dominant role, to metaphorically storm the castle (with bullying or controlling or abusive behaviours), or it triggers others to coddle or protect or rescue. It typically does not engender admiration or respect or appreciation.

It turns out that our medieval metaphor has a lot of scope, doesn't it? To completely exhaust the analogy, it is no better to have the natural-born ruler overthrown and usurped by a war-mongering, bloodthirsty tyrant than it is to have an impotent, apprehensive ruler who is little more than a figurehead, shadowed by sycophants, and open to manipulation like a puppet on a string. You've seen *Game of Thrones*. You know what I'm talking about.

So with regard to our couple and their young son, a "no" parental approach could be akin to the Mad King scaling the turrets and establishing rule on the basis of fear. Our father was telling his son to "do as you're told" for no other reason than it was what he was told. "Respect my authority because I have been ordained with authority" is an authoritarian approach. On the flip side, a "yes" parental approach can be akin to the queen mother skulking about in the shadows, murmuring words that foster dependency and self-doubt. Our mother would undermine her husband and offer reassurances to her son like "Don't listen to that" or "Daddy gets really angry doesn't he? We don't need to listen to him." In other words, "Follow my authority, because I will treat you nice and kind and sweet, oh child of mine."

While these archetypes are psychological caricatures, they do represent, at a somewhat farcical level, the roles that ordinary, everyday people assume within the drama of their own lives. The psychological paradox of it all was endlessly confusing to Dad—but yet, when you understand the human psyche, there is no contradiction or confusion at all. It is a tale as old as time. Every human being seeks for empowerment from a place of disempowerment. It is the hero's journey. On the one hand, if the atmosphere is saturated in coddling and rescuing, a psychological current of collaboration is frequently established; conversely, a deeper psychological undercurrent of rebellion is equally and oppositely established. This is all to say that our father, while on the one hand professing helpfulness and agreeableness and wanting to please his wife, on the other hand evidenced deeper currents of resentment and anger. This was particularly directed towards his son.

Dad—Disempowered Tame—Like a Docile Little Kitten
Coddling = Current of Collaboration
(On the Surface: People Pleasing and Amenable, a Yes-Man)

+

Coddling = Deeper Current of Rebellion
(Under the Surface: Harsh and Critical and Hopeless)
Seeks Confidence (But May Find Unskilled
Confidence as Aggression)

This father often found himself with an irresistible urge to throw off niceties in an effort to reclaim his power, but what he gained was not controlled power, not wise power, not true power, but a kind of counterfeit power—uncontrolled power, aggression. This psychological story was exactly the same as his son's. The boy was groping about trying to strike his own personal balance in the midst of Dad's imbalance and Mum's imbalance too.

Within the marital relationship, Dad's sweetness and friendliness and niceness, while often sincere, could become meekness devoid of strength, like a docile little kitten. Disempowerment begets disempowerment begets disempowerment. Bear in mind that we are always talking about the nuances of the human psyche. While obviously these dynamics can go to extremes, they are more often played out in very subtle ways. Always remember as well that we are discussing these dynamics in terms of psychological health and psychological empowerment. If you will recall, I myself have been guilty of meekness devoid of strength. This meekness is born of social conditioning rather than true empowerment. It is a lack of confidence and low self-esteem. While it can appear good on the surface it has the hallmarks of conformity rather than empowerment.

Neither people-pleasing nor controlling behaviours are, in and of themselves, good or bad. Rather, it all comes back to degrees of empowerment. Empowered meekness is one of the quintessential features of many of the world's renowned spiritual leaders. But there needs be an artful balance between meek and assertive, directive and non-directive, collaborative and independent, wild and tame.

So let us move along and take a look at my client's mother. An atmosphere steeped in cossetting and overprotection often fosters resentment thinly veiled in people-pleasing, while an atmosphere drenched in authoritative control or heavy-handed restrictions builds up a psychological current of rebellion. As we saw in the first chapter, rebellion against authority can have the flavour of empowerment; indeed, nonconformity is often the first step towards true empowerment. However, rebellion for rebellion's sake remains a far cry from the genuine article.

True empowerment is a journey of many steps, and we would not sojourn five kilometres into a hundred-kilometre journey and rejoice that our travels were over. We will discuss in more depth how rebellion and anger and nonconformity have their value, but for now, let it suffice to say that a wild nature is psychologically very healthy, but a savage nature is not. A tame nature is psychologically very beneficial, but an impotent nature is not. So while a punitive atmosphere can foster rebellion, there remains a deeper psychological undercurrent established with equal but opposite vigour.

Mum—Disempowered Wild—Like a Ferocious Lion
Punitive = Current of Rebellion
(On the Surface: Critical and Irritable)

+

Punitive = Deeper Current of Collaboration
(Under the Surface: Amenable and Kind)
Seeks Kindness (but May Find Unskilled Kindness as Impotence)

People-pleasers look to be adept at confidence, but they may find themselves in danger of unskilled confidence at times—that is, aggression. Within the marital relationship this mother had become defensive and oppositional. Towards her son she demonstrated endless patience and boundless empathy. But with her husband in her sights she became more like a ferocious lion. She floundered in her efforts to strike the artful balance between assertiveness and submission, empowered kindness, confident acquiescence. Such individuals may find themselves in danger of unskilled acquiescence—being a doormat. This is all to say that in the example of our mother, while on the one hand she appeared to nag and domineer, being ostensibly harsh and critical with her husband, there were deeper currents of compassion and concern and helpfulness that were accentuated in her relationship with her son but withheld in her relationship with her husband.

She too often found herself with an irresistible urge to throw off the heavy and suffocating cloak of antagonism in her efforts to reclaim her power of collaboration, but as was the case with Dad, it was not genuine power, not wise power, not authentic power, but a kind of counterfeit power. Rather than be "bitchy," she would become limp and ineffectual in the name of collaboration. It was collaboration to appease. It was defeated acquiescence.

Again, this psychological story was exactly the same as her son's. This child's psychological dilemma, as it related to Dad, was that he was overly rebellious (though at deep levels wanting to be more amenable);

however, when it came to Mum, he could be overly dependent, a "mummy's boy" as it were (though at a deeper level he wanted to be more assertive). Disempowerment begets disempowerment begets disempowerment. Are we stretching those psychological muscles yet?

On the surface, we believe that we want people to agree with us. I can imagine many mothers reading our example and thinking, "Oh, I wish I had a husband who tried to please me. Even if he was just trying, I'd appreciate that. This woman has it so good. She should live with my husband for a week!" We deeply believe that if we were surrounded by yes-men, life would be more joyful and easier. We would be happier if we were agreed with and pleased. However, this idea of utopia, this nirvana, does not allow for spiritual and psychological growth.

Empowerment necessarily entails some degree of assertiveness and self-actualisation. It must contain some facet of authentic individualisation. At the deepest of spiritual and psychological levels, we want to own and express our unique, personal voice, and when we sense that somebody is mollycoddling us, we become psychologically imbalanced. Put simply, dominance seeks to be imbued with a dash of submission, and submission seeks a healthy dollop of dominance.

A personality like this mother (and this father at various times) who is encouraged to remain dominant, bossy, arrogant, or self-righteous actually begins to lose wisdom because she begins to lose balance. She grows in wild attributes but, to some extent, more tame qualities begin to fade. As people begin to lose balance, they appear to onlookers more as one-dimensional caricature than as well-rounded, nuanced characters. At a deep spiritual and psychological level, this type of personality begins to ask for or call forth qualities in a mate that have the potential to restore balance. To say it a different way, people who have started to embed themselves in confidence can easily fall into overconfidence. There is a fine line between assertive and aggressive. They can begin to neglect their more humble qualities, and those muscles atrophy through lack of use.

Have you ever encountered a strong personality who has a fierce talent for assertiveness? This is the type of person you would imagine as CEO of a major corporation or a strong matriarch of a family system. Have you ever noticed how often people with this type of personality, while intimidating to many, seem to respect and appreciate somebody who can meet them at their level of self-empowerment? Rather than being offended by disagreeable colleagues, they often seem to revel in hearty debate with somebody who is not seeking to please them but rather be authentic with them. This mutually beneficial relationship allows one to foster humility while the other fosters confidence.

Now, I am well aware that there are exceptions to this general rule. Remember, I am not talking in absolutes. But I hope you understand the point I'm making. Just as an overly dominant wife can actually call forth ever-increasing submissive attributes from her partner, so too can an overly submissive mother begin to elicit more and more dominant qualities within a son. It is psychologically healthy to learn the hallmarks of a wild nature, like assertiveness and independence and confidence, *and* to learn the hallmarks of a tame nature, like kindness and collaboration and compassion in equal measure.

In broad terms, it is psychologically optimal for an individual to understand and conform to the human rules and expectations of planet Earth—such as driving on the right side of the road and paying taxes and not stealing—because, after all, life is lived in human form and on human terms. However, the divine nature is highly individualised and independent and free-thinking and nonconformist. Finding this balance point and living within this constant tension is the art of life and can only be done successfully when individuals are given greater scope to decide the extent to which conformity is personally appropriate for them. It is the yin and the yang at the heart of everything. Light and dark, wild and tame, interpersonally as well as intrapersonally.

If this chapter has seemed confusing or has given you a psychological hernia, then sit and relax. Don't do any strenuous mental exercise, but read on, because I will reiterate these principles many times and in many different ways so that you will come to completely understand and appreciate how they relate to parental relationships, marital relationships, sibling relationships, and the most important relationship of all: the relationship between you and You.

CHAPTER 3

Kids are the Psychological Masters Amongst Us

My favourite metaphor to tell kids who are considered difficult or who are, themselves, experiencing difficulty within their own life experience is this: Imagine that you are walking with a lion or wolf or a dragon beside you. Imagine how magnificent you would appear to onlookers—to walk with such a spectacular beast or to have this mythic creature at your flank. Now imagine if this animal were wild! Not only would other people be terrified at your approach, but you, yourself, would be troubled. While yes, this lion or dragon or wolf may be let loose upon your enemies and vanquish them in spectacular fashion, it may also maul an innocent bystander at any moment. This dragon may indiscriminately set fire to castle and village! When untrained and un-tame, such a beast may turn and attack you, its owner. To walk with such a potent creature is the stuff of great myth, but it is a power that needs to be wielded wisely.

I had the recent privilege of speaking to a teenage girl who perfectly epitomised this tension between wild and tame natures. She had a long and chequered mental-health history. She had experienced great intensity of emotion across her lifetime, from despair to rage to profound insight and deep compassion. She had come to me after being released from hospital for a suicide attempt, something of which she had considerable experience. While in hospital, she had apparently caused quite a ruckus, so much so that hospital staff were agreeable when early discharge was discussed.

I couldn't help but visualise the lioness at her flank. I imagined that she would give the beast an emphatic, knowing nod before letting it loose upon the poor doctors and nurses. I pictured them running the halls as the sheer power of this young woman's determination and defiance struck them full force, effectively overpowering and mauling them. As I articulated this to my young client, she offered an impish grin. She knew deeply that she was a force to be reckoned with. She held within her the power of a tornado—creative, but in a destructive way. She resonated deeply with this conceptualisation and recognised the spiritual essence of it.

Within the depths of her being, she knew and could verbalise her sense of purpose. Her wild nature was serving her in powerful ways. In fact, she was able to access more breadth and depth of power within herself that a whole roomful of adults, who were intimidated or confounded by her. While loathe to admit to this intimidation, adults preferred to admonish her, hence her early discharge. Children are not supposed to be more savvy and more powerful and more wise, you see.

Her wild nature was her doorway to deep instinct and profound insights. This magnificent young woman had gone to great pains to prove to herself that she was here for great meaning and purpose. Indeed, some of her more emphatic suicide attempts were about exactly that. However, as beneficial as these wild attributes were, they could also be the stuff of great torment. While her suicide attempts, on an epic scale, could be thought of as the classic heroine's journey down to Hades, the question remained: in a life and death battle with the monsters of the psyche, how do you know when it's you defeating the monster and not the monster defeating you? Suicide attempts are often self-directed anger, a tortured and troubled mind imploding rather than exploding. While, yes, power is inherent within both implosion and explosion, it would ultimately be psychologically better to channel this force into constructive endeavours rather than destructive ones. This is what I mean when I say that a wild nature can become savage.

For a parent, the analogy of the lion or dragon aptly describes the raising of a wild child. It can also accurately describe the experience of being wild also. However, counter to traditional psychology, I would never want to problemise this nature. I would certainly never pathologise this nature. Rather, I believe that awakened psychology can assist parents to help kids tame these most confident, bold, strong traits. This is what these innate qualities are: confidence, not arrogance, and independence, not defiance.

When all is said and done, isn't this why we revere dragons and lions and wolves and phoenixes? They represent confidence and empowerment. This is the essence of a kid's spiritual nature, not their anti-spiritual nature. Just think about the absurdity of insisting that fiercely independent children just do as they're told. It is literally the case that when such a child says no, the adult is now wandering into dangerous territory. Isn't it parents' own fierce independence and confidence about their own opinion and resistance to being controlled that pits them against a child who says no in the first place?

As we explored together in the first chapter, when a child is essentially saying "I want the right to *have* my own opinion and *trust* my own opinion," an antagonistic adult is also essentially saying, "Well, I want the right to hold to *my* own opinion, and I trust *my* own opinion too." Stalemate! As in the case of most power struggles, it's the bigger, stronger, more highly resourced side that would appear to win—at least in physical, action terms, but fortunately not in spiritual terms.

The young woman I mentioned perfectly personified this battle of wills. She had long ago refused traditional education and was negotiating her way through more unconventional avenues. Whichever traditional institution she encountered—be it education, medicine, or even psychology—she would come up against notions of conformity and adults who seemed to insist that, by virtue of their age and experience, they knew better. In part, I would like this book to not only imbue modern parenting with a more psychologically accurate basis but also lead us to be more spiritually savvy in our parenting.

I find it intriguing to talk to people about their spirituality and observe how this spiritual nature is infused into daily life. Just to offer you a brief forecast, I hold similar ideas about traditional religion as I do about traditional psychology and traditional education. To put it bluntly, I believe that we are evolving into a new age of enlightenment whereby personal spirituality will supersede conventional religion, and it will begin to divorce itself from limiting concepts and restrictive edicts. I believe that we are in the midst of a shift in mass consciousness, and the pillars are crumbling down about us. Into this void, I would like to suggest that eternal spiritual truths could be woven into our parenting, and all would be the better for it.

So back to my initial statement, when talking to people about their religious beliefs, I am often left perplexed and curious. I ask myself, "What does *spirit* actually mean to this person?" It is from this seedbed that much of my psychological understanding has sprouted and bloomed. It is my strong conviction that we are spirit first and foremost. The teachers and gurus and yogis and masters that I most respect and admire have embodied this tenet in their lives. A namaste consciousness honours the quintessential spiritual nature within self and other. As Pierre Teilhard de Chardin wrote, "We are not human beings having a spiritual experience. We are spiritual beings having a human experience."

So how have we applied this fundamental spiritual truth to psychology and, by extension, to our notions of parenting? Not very well, if at all, in my opinion. When the discipline of psychology was in its infancy, notions of the self were not necessarily well evolved. Psychology grew up in a time where thought was king and the physical universe was legitimised. It was a time of autopsies within medicine, rocket ships within astrophysics, warring within politics. The offshoot of all this was that more masculine traits and talents were esteemed: intellect, ingenuity, problem-solving, negotiation, organisation, structure, order, control, discipline. Within the quaternity of the human psyche—thought, physical (action), emotional, and spiritual— the first two aspects were isolated and venerated. The resulting diminishment of emotional and spiritual characteristics has left modern psychology imbalanced and incomplete. The more feminine traits have historically been derided, in line with women themselves, and within this social petri dish we have grown a specific problem.

The rational, the practical, the logical, and the sensible hold great sway within Western culture—in our psychology, in our education, in our politics, in our medicine, and in our sciences. There is little room given to the intuitive, the instinctual, the ineffable, the mysterious, the unquantifiable, the emotional, and the spiritual. I will talk in a later chapter about how, given the environment of its formative years, psychology is clearly biased even within its diagnostic system, but for now I would like to just set the scene for you. For now, let it suffice to say that this prejudice hinders what could otherwise be a deep and profound understanding of human nature. So what does any of this have to do with kids and parenting? Good question. Everything!

To say that Western psychology has largely devalued the emotional is fair; to say that Western psychology has largely devalued the spiritual is an understatement. At a systemic level, this inclination has been so pervasive that we have consequently formed social concepts about what it is to be successfully human. Think about what our idea of successfully raising a child entails. In essence, across childhood, kids are trained away from naughty and trained towards nice. This sound fair enough, doesn't it? But look a bit closer and you will notice that often this literally means training kids away from their emotional/spiritual orientation and training them towards their thought/physical proclivities.

Let me give you an easy example to make the point a bit clearer. When children, especially young children, are at their most heightened emotionally, we often deem them to be naughty or wrong. This is what we refer to when we say they are having a tantrum. They are in an intensely emotional state and, from the ivory tower of adulthood, we decide that they need to be stopped or at the very least subdued. Think about it. In Australia's school systems we have the classic behavioural modification program "Stop, Think, Do." There are no programs called "Feel, Intuit, Sense." This perfectly epitomises the fact that a successful transition from toddlerhood into childhood is regarded as a shift away from intense emotional expressions towards more restrained thought expressions (never mind spiritual expressions).

If you have ever watched any episodes of *Supernanny*, you will know that a young child in the midst of an intense emotional experience, be it anger or disappointment or even elation or ecstasy or invincibility, is encouraged to sit quietly and think about what he or she has done. Sit and think, sit and think, sit and think. No more of that noisy, unacceptable emotion stuff. I know that's putting it in strong terms, but to varying degrees, it is common. Without fail, every parent I encounter echoes this philosophy. Children who are regarded as overly emotional are considered by adults to be ill-equipped to manoeuvre their way successfully through life. Adults are intimidated by emotion or perplexed by it or afraid of it. Even when speaking with my adult clients about their depression or anxiety or anger a large portion of my work is simply normalising emotion to people. I frequently find myself reassuring adults that their intense emotional experience does not mean they are going crazy.

Life—that is, the "life" that is currently done on adult terms—is entirely thought-oriented. In a thought-dominated culture, somebody who is highly emotional can flounder. It can even be the case that an emotionally oriented teen who has retained these beautiful and magnificent emotional and/or spiritual talents is mocked for being childish—"sook," "baby," "mummy's boy," "pussy." Efforts are made to train the emotional out of kids. They are thought of as too weak, too sensitive, too intense, and too soft.

With eerie consistency, all the parents I talk to try to coach their children away from the emotional by discussing feelings. They work hard to introduce thought into the feeling equation, often commenting to me:

"I ask her what's wrong."

"I've asked him to explain it to me."

"He can't tell me what is the matter."

"She doesn't know what it's about."

In subtle but insidious ways, we adults seek to converse about emotions. We try to intellectualise and justify and explain and reason our way through them. Even putting language to emotion is a subtle way that thought is introduced; it's like dropping a fine gossamer blanket of thought over the top of feelings. The fabric is so light and so fine that it is almost imperceptible, but it's there.

Once children have received this basic training in Thinking Your Way through Feelings 101, they graduate into tween- and teen-hood. Now we expect kids to largely be grown out of intense emotional expressions, and our language is peppered with judgement-laden phraseology like "He's got a good head on his shoulders," "He has really thought this through," or "She just doesn't think." Success for teenagers, in adult terms, is often based upon how indoctrinated they've become, how well they've acclimated to social norms, how well they can reason about drugs and alcohol, how well they can rationalise about their future, and how well they can apply discipline and self-control regarding sex—think, think, think, think, think. The crux of all of this is that when you try to exorcise a natural and powerful aspect of personhood - emotion - by implying that it's superfluous or substandard, you create a generation who still feels, but feels bad about feeling.

We cannot rid ourselves of the emotional experience. People still feel the same way people have always felt, but we have become unfamiliar with our own emotional landscape. We no longer bring wisdom and insight to our emotional experience. This is part of the reason why we have generations of kids overwhelmed by depression or anxiety. Typical and understandable emotions like sadness and fear are left to fester, with conventional wisdom offering little more than "Let's just think about this," "Reason your way through it," "Explain it to someone," or "Take a pill, it's just like any other physical ailment." Even psychology, in its more recent incarnations, still has vestiges of this rationalisation approach, and I will discuss the nuance of this in more detail in a later chapter.

So what would happen if we were to flip the paradigm? What if the psychological process of growing up were seen more for what it is: a training away from overly emotional demonstrations? If we were to scrutinise this psychological process more thoroughly to understand its inherent pitfalls, we might come to appreciate that kids are, in fact, the psychological masters amongst us.

If you profess yourself to be spiritual or religious, it seems fair to assume that, to some degree, you ascribe to the notion that we are spirit first and foremost. Even if your religious understanding extends simply to the premise that a soulful Self will depart the body after death and fly off to a distant, ethereal realm, it seems appropriate to presume that you believe yourself to *now* be in possession of such a soulful Self in order for this belief to have any internal logic. It also seems reasonable to presume that you would agree to the eternal nature of this soulful Self. So if the human experience is inextricably linked somehow to spiritual experience (and indeed it is), and if the soul, or spirit, is eternal (and we agree on that), it would seem logical that infancy provides us with the clearest vision of a pure, unencumbered human/spirit intermingling.

Let me say that in a slightly different way for the sake of clarity. I have gone to considerable length within the pages of this book to point out and explain to you a few of the many and varied ways that society constructs the human psyche around clear, discernable ideologies. We have looked at some constructs pertaining to kids specifically and some pertaining to people generally. I will take for granted here that you have been swayed by some of these arguments, or that you came to this material already appreciating how society got a hold of your mind at a very early age and started to skew and mould it. So if an infant entering into this physical reality trailing the stuff of heaven (eternal, remember) assumes physical form as a human being (human and spirit intimately linked, remember), then this infant should represent super-spirituality, uber-spirituality, spirituality on steroids. Right?

I would go so far as to say that, if you have children or even if you've been close to an infant, you already know this deep spiritual truth, but you have perhaps not conceptualised it in this way before. By and large, adults have a natural reverence for infants. We talk more quietly around them. We handle them like precious china. We smell them, we marvel at them, and we take endless photos of them. We are in awe of how precious and perfect and pristine and unblemished they are. This is our sprit in recognition of and homage to its Self.

"And then they grow up," I hear you chuckle. Once society has had its way with us, we commonly *stop* questioning and critiquing and criticising obviously fear-based ideologies. We are trained so expertly to go along and be sensible. We so easily do what is expected that we find ourselves working in jobs we don't enjoy, socialising with people we don't like, discriminating against a whole nation or religious group, buying products we don't need, and fearing germs and feelings and sharks and Muslims and failure and death and workplace injury and … and … and … and.

It's like a seemingly innocuous substance is injected into our bloodstream at birth and lies dormant until the age of about five to seven, when it is activated and slowly, imperceptibly, begins to affect our eyesight by infusing everything with a slight, subtle red hue. By age nine to eleven, the substance has started to take noticeable effect, and our vision is clouded over with this faint red hue. By age thirteen to fifteen, some individuals experience a minor halting in the effect and can see things in a noticeably different way than their adult counterparts. However, if things progress in a typical fashion, the substance has taken full effect upon the majority of the population by the age of seventeen to nineteen and the red hue is firmly in place.

The reason for this somewhat sci-fi analogy is to emphasise the fact that kids, for a time, stand outside of societal norms. This is not a disadvantage to them; it is to their supreme advantage! When society is so skewed that somebody like Donal Trump can garner significant support as a presidential candidate in America you know that many adults are not necessarily seeing that clearly. We are in the throes of a psychological, tectonic shift, and in my opinion, kids are the teachers, not necessarily the other way around.

The psychological mastery and spiritual savvy that kids possess is clear to the well-trained eye. It is perceptible and detectable. For a start, kids are happier! This may seem blatantly obvious and hardly in need of recognition, but I would suggest to you that it is precisely *because* this fact is so writ large that the Western adult population has lost sight of it. We take happiness to be the whimsical, naïve hallmark of childhood. We ascribe this degree of happiness to those fond, long-forgotten days of yore. As adults, we easily lose sight of the spiritual and psychological profundities of the childlike and ridicule them as childish.

Adults can be so proud and self-righteous and, to be frank, brainwashed that within their own minds maturity is reasonably synonymous with grumpiness, worry, stress, and responsibility. You know the sentiment that I'm referring to: it's that old catch-cry, "It's okay for you to be care free and happy, you obviously don't pay the bills around here." It's like a morbid, grotesque badge of honour that we wear within our tribe, the tribe whose elders proudly hang the scorched bones of the martyr around their necks. "Sure I'm miserable, sure I'm overworked, sure I'm stressed and exhausted, sure I'll drink too much, sure I'll want to have an affair, sure I'll be angry, I may even want to kill myself ... but it's just what we adults *need* to do."

It's like, long ago, within our tribe, we performed the sacred rituals and took the death march up to the volcano's edge. We clattered the bones and rattled the skulls of the martyr. We sacrificed "happy" to the demigod of "responsibility." Before kids get to an age where guilt and shame have taken hold, they can orient themselves easily to happiness. Even when they have become unhappy, they can often reorient themselves with little help or interference from adults. This, my dear friends, is psychological mastery! It is not just psychological mastery, it is spiritual mastery. This is what it is.

The thousands of people who have come to me over my decade of work as a clinical psychologist have been seeking this singular prize. People want to be happier than they are, and yet when happiness is personified right before their eyes, that icky red hue prevents clear sight. I know, I know, I can hear your protests. I've heard it all before. People can easily dismiss my words—and do, because they tell themselves things like "What does she know?" or "Sure, that's fine if you're a psychologist," or "I'm not just gonna quit my job," or "Yeah, yeah, *happy* ... that'll pay my bills, you crazy lady."

Firstly, that last comment was a bit harsh, and secondly I am not advocating for childish behaviour. Don't stumble into that dualistic thinking trap again. Remember that advocating for one position does not mean that I am denouncing its opposite. Of course you are going to honour your commitments to your employer and your creditors, and of course you need to earn money to pay for the necessities of life. These necessities are as essential to your life in human form as anything else. We are in agreement. I obviously get that. What I am in favour of are *childlike* qualities, not *childish* qualities. The acuities of childhood do not mean that we should stay as children even into adulthood; that is not spiritually or psychologically masterful. But we can honour and admire the psychological treasures of childhood and carry these gems with us into adulthood as best we can.

In addition to happiness, children—especially before the age of five or six—demonstrate wonderful emotional authenticity, spectacular confidence, consummate tolerance and acceptance, and excellent individuality and uniqueness. They also, you've probably noticed, have a very free and open relationship with their emotions. Emotional expression is not an issue for a three-year-old. Young children, and particularly sensitive older children, are so skilled in the emotional arenas that, as much as society has renounced the importance of feminine traits, they are a double offense for children. At lease adulthood affords women some degree of power and authority, some validation. Nothing of value or wisdom is expected to come forth from a child, so much so that children were to be seen and not heard during periods of our history. Yet children, having recently come forth into physical existence, are innately enlightened and empowered, and they hold firm to that for a time.

It's like they decide to set out upon a grand adventure, an epic quest. They come forth carrying the proverbial accent of their mother tongue—gentleness, confidence, freedom, joy, adventure, spontaneity, acceptance, uniqueness, and boldness. Love, in its many forms, is their native language. Their homeland is obviously a wonderful place because what they exude through their being is delightful, an elixir for those of us who still remember home. But when you travel to a foreign land, you must find your bearings. Our grown-up system is so contrary to what they remember of their homeland that kids become discombobulated. It's like moving to a country that does not speak your language and needing to learn how to communicate anew.

Infants are birthed into a system where not only is thought given greater sway, but fear-based thought is prevalent and legitimised.

Children are indeed wanderers in a strange land. As they seek only to feel acceptance and love, they are cautioned to be wary and suspicious. As they seek only to feel trust in their own instincts and enable their innate greatness, they are rebuked for naivety and lack of humility. As they seek only to feel confident in their own mind and express their own perspectives, they are chastised for arrogance and selfishness.

However, if you would cast your mind back a few decades, you would recall that you were five years old once. While you may have learned, just like your children did, that "here in this place, we… do.… fear, we do hard, we do struggle," you too are still an expatriate. You may have picked up the language here, you may have learned the system of law and convention, you may even have fallen in love with the place as you intended when you set out upon your grand adventure. But you will never lose your accent. Even when you are thinking those fear-filled thoughts, the lilting accent of love is there; even when you are speaking those discouraged ideas, that symphonic accent of love is there; even when you are acting out those angry biases, that exquisite accent of love is there. It is omnipresent and omniscient.

Oh wait, I know something else that has those qualities too. Children are the angels amongst us, and we have cast them as the little devils. While you might take the angel out of heaven, you will never take heaven out of the angel. Children do spiritual and psychological mastery simply because they have not forgotten how.

The cornerstone of this proficiency is their innate and instinctive understanding of emotion. Children are emotion-beings. They are like emotional barometers, and they can take a reading of whatever emotional atmosphere they find themselves in. Adults can often disregard the splendour of this sense-ability, this psychic aptitude, because they have forgotten that this capacity lies dormant within them also. If you have been banging about in a foreign land for three score and ten, it's fair to say that the memories of home have probably grown dim and distant. Kids up until about four years old are largely untroubled by their emotional experiences, however intense. While adults around them may be freaking out on their behalf—or worse, reprimanding them—very young children can usually remain quite psychologically buoyant in spite of their parents. They haven't picked up on the strange, alien language we adults all seem to speak (and quite frankly, they have no desire to).

Once society at large gets a hold of them, they are given many mixed signals about which emotions are good and which are bad. They are bombarded with messages about what emotions mean and what to do with them. The seeds of self-doubt or confusion or guilt are planted, and later this weed plot will be psychologically designated; depression or anxiety.

CHAPTER 4

As Adults, We Are Overly Familiar with Anxiety and Depression

Throughout my career, I have held many different professional opinions and utilised many different techniques and modalities. I would like to think that my practice has evolved in line with my own personal journey of empowerment and enlightenment. I used to believe that honouring feelings was necessary and in fact paramount, and I still very strongly believe that, although I think my ideas about what I am honouring have evolved.

As I mentioned in the previous chapter, our Western culture has become highly skewed towards thought and action. The intellect (masculine) has been idolised while the instinct (feminine) has been moderated. Subsequently, we have become a very smart culture but not necessarily a very wise one. Our journey back to the wisdom and empowerment dwelling within the emotional landscape is prudent and vital; however, contrary to some of my colleagues, I would probably survey the emotional landscape with an eye for the beautiful. I'm typically on the lookout for the oasis in the parched desert. I don't want to overspeak or overanalyse or overthink negative emotions.

Don't get me wrong—I believe that being at peace with feelings like anxiety or depression is extremely important. Bringing an air of acceptance to emotions like worry and sadness is great. Indeed, I am often struck by how many clients I see who, having only recently experienced the death of a loved one, are prescribed antidepressant medication. A normal grief response is medicalised and sometimes even termed "adjustment disorder" in medical notes. Too often we medicate grief, arguably one of the most understandable emotional reactions of all.

In Western society, we have a very low tolerance for uncomfortable or confronting emotions, and we feel easily overwhelmed when circumstances stretch us outside of our typical emotional comfort zones. We are like kids playing in the street right outside of the house. We feel safe when we stick close to home, and neutral emotions or slightly negative or slightly positive emotions feel like home base. It's safe to play around in these feelings, skipping over the back fence to see the neighbour boy two streets behind or wandering to the park only a couple of streets over to play with the Jameson twins. But once we've detoured into unfamiliar emotional territory, we feel lost.

I have often had clients tell me they feel like they are "going crazy" or that their negative feelings "will never stop." Intense negative emotions or even very strong positive emotions can feel overwhelming and terrifying or unnerving. While I would like us to be at peace with any and all emotions as a necessary starting point, now I am more inclined to move the conversation along—not because of my own impatience, and not because I don't care. Here is why I do it: we have become overly familiar with anxiety and depression in our culture.

I know that it may seem like I am contradicting myself. On the one hand, I am saying that the whole gamut of the human emotional experience is okay, and on the other hand, I seem to be saying that anxiety and depression aren't okay—we're overly familiar with them. As with all facets of psychological mastery, it's a question of balance. I believe that traditional psychology has often been a culprit for overly indulging negative emotions. I would even have considered myself guilty of this, to an extent, not that long ago. Now I find myself contemplating where the line is between acceptance and indulgence. When I meet somebody in their disempowerment, it is a necessary meeting point, to be sure, but I ask myself: how skilfully and artfully can I coax this individual into empowerment?

When I speak to clients about an empowered focus to therapy, I often find myself using this analogy: Imagine you have been thrust into a pitch-black dungeon. You are terrified and confused and helpless. In an effort to establish some semblance of normalcy and control, you begin to feel around the dark chamber. You feel the moist, dank stonework; you feel the contours and gradations. Sometimes you feel the crumble and hear the chink of the mortar grit that falls to the ground. Your fingers meander across a hole or indentation, and you make a mental note: "Five hand lengths from the back right-hand corner, three hand widths from the ground."

Day after day, month after month you console yourself with the mental map you are making of your prison cell. This is what traditional psychology and traditional psychiatry and traditional medicine are like: groping about in the darkness trying to describe the qualities of the darkness, the contours of the darkness, the pungent odours of the darkness. When did the darkness first begin? Why did the darkness first begin? Whose fault is this darkness? What might we do about it?

For a time, this may seem helpful. There is certainly some value in psychoanalysis and psychotherapy when it's a catalyst for transformation and revelation. For me personally, however, I would prefer to bring in the light. You may not think so, but this can be a tricky thing. When people feel trapped in a dark hole or a dank dungeon, they often begin to adjust to their prison. Sometimes psychological empowerment can feel like swinging open the cell door and flooding the oubliette with light. A long-time prisoner of the dungeon will cower against this light. The magnitude and intensity of such brightness literally feels blinding. The prisoner might beg, "Close the door! Close the door!" The skill and art of empowered psychology is about allowing single points of light to cascade into the darkness— just enough to illuminate, enough to in-lighten, but not too much, not too much to cringe against.

One of my more recent clients is a great illustration of this. In my earlier days as a psychologist, I dutifully performed my initial session as I was taught. It was essentially a formulation of an individual's psychosocial influences, past and present. Things like current relationships, childhood experiences, work history, developmental and medical histories, and past drug or alcohol use were discussed. It was like taking a snapshot of significant details (well, what was deemed significant by prevailing standards). I did it well, and I know it was cathartic for many clients.

More recently I have been bypassing—or perhaps modifying is a better word—this formulation to a certain extent because it can be like groping about in the darkness. It's the "So how and why have you ended up in this cell?" approach. Now I try to balance this history-taking with discussions about the light:

"What about when life was going really well for you?"

"Tell me about your strengths, what are the traits you really like about yourself?"

"When do you feel most confident? Talk to me about that."

One of my more recent clients provides a classic example of how some people can be baffled by a psychologist who wants to discuss the proverbial light. Once I had ascertained a fuzzy, but sufficient, picture of the darkness as it related to this particular client, I headed straight for an investigation about the light. With each question, my client wanted to circle back to explain and rationalise and justify the hole she was in.

"So when life was going along very well, what was that like?" I would ask.

"Oh good, much better than now, but now it's bad," she would reply.

"So if it's bad now, what does good look like for you, the opposite of now?"

"Oh yes, absolutely, I used to be more resilient and more confident, but not anymore."

"Could you explain what you're like when you're confident? What helps you feel resilient?"

"Oh yes, it's good, much better than now, but I don't feel that way now."

Around and around we went, not with any displeasure or annoyance on my part (I'm not sure about her), but patiently. It is simply the necessary, subtle unravelling process—unravelling expectations and beliefs, including a belief that analysing the hole helps one get out of it and an expectation that one should explain the hole one is in before it's okay to climb out.

In my own personal experiences with life, I too have felt that suffering was necessary. It was to be anticipated, and analysis ostensibly served in the healing process. I sought to normalise my own dungeon experiences—feelings like fear, sadness, and anger. I set about normalising negative emotions simply because I often felt these feelings too.

I wanted to understand myself, and my training had taught me that formulating the *why* and *how* and *who* and *when* was beneficial. To a point, it was indeed. There is some empowerment to be mined in these places. I also wanted to bring the self-compassion and self-kindness to others that I had found for myself. Don't get me wrong; this approach was great and helpful, and I am still an advocate for kind non-judgement of whatever emotions show up. Nevertheless, as Eckhart Tolle says, "Suffering is necessary until you realise it is unnecessary." I have come to realise in a powerful way that feelings like anxiety or depression or anger are not normal but have been normalised.

I know for many that statement may be hard to hear and might make them defensive. You may vehemently assure me of the fact that emotions like sadness or anger happen for you, and this alone makes them normal. To a degree, I concede that any aspect of the human experience is normal by virtue of its inclusion as a part of the human experience. It's like a self-fulfilling prophesy, a circular argument that affirms itself. It's normal, so I feel it, and I feel it, so it's normal. Perhaps *normal* is too much of a loaded word. I know anger, sadness, and fear happen—I'm human, of course I get that—but I believe we have become overly familiar with these feelings and come to anticipate them, overly much, as part of the journey. There is a vast difference between honouring whatever emotion shows up and indulging whatever feelings show up.

Let us remind ourselves of our psychological and spiritual consorts. Kids can wade through more intense emotional experiences than adults. They don't just feel sad, they feel miserable: "I've had the worst day ever, everybody hates me, I had nobody to play with, my life sucks, I'm not going back." They don't just feel happy, they feel exuberant: "Today was brilliant, it was so funny, and I played with Sally, but then she went to play with Joanna, and I played hopscotch, and then Rebecca said we should play hide and seek, and then, and then, and, but, um, my teacher gave me another merit point, are we having these sausages for dinner?" There may be higher peaks and lower troughs, but the duration of negative emotion is much shorter and the general mood is more in harmony with positive emotions, especially in very young children.

On balance, young kids are more often joyful and optimistic. They can ride the wave of their emotions much more proficiently, and the natural ebb and flow bothers them little. I'm sure you have seen kids just like I have, maybe up close if you've got your own kids and maybe at a distance. You know as well as I that they can emotionally spin on a dime. I have three children, and my six-year-old and four-year-old often fight like cats and dogs. When I make a deliberate effort to interfere as little as possible, I am astonished at times. My six-year-old son may be tormenting my four-year-old daughter. She is screaming that high-pitched banshee yowl that seems to come as an inbuilt feature with little girls. She is so loud that I worry the neighbours will think we have strapped her to a medieval torture device, and then suddenly the most miraculous thing happens. My son, quite accidentally, does something that is hilarious to my daughter. Now she is vacillating between giggles and half-hearted whimpers. She can't decide between guffaws and gripes. Then all of a sudden, like thunder clapping after lightening, laughter shoots out. Despite herself, she is happy again.

Nearly without exception, every person I speak with failed to learn to treasure and protect positive emotions. At the same time, people often argue for the validity and legitimacy of their negative emotions. "Let's see if we can say that in a more hopeful way," I suggest.

"Yes, but the situation isn't hopeful," they reply.

"Maybe we can tell the story in a more hopeful way," I recommend.

"Yes, but this is wrong, and this is wrong, and this is wrong. That's why I don't feel hopeful," they scoff.

"Perhaps we can think more hopefully just for the benefit of hopefulness," I suggest.

"Yes, but I'm angry because of this, I'm frustrated because of that," they say and proceed to smack me upside the head (only kidding).

Sometimes I speak with clients who say that they have been feeling good and weren't sure whether they needed to come and see me. This sentiment often reveals to me two very interesting things:

1. People believe that you see a psychologist to do "problem talk."
2. People do not give nearly as much effort or attention to positive feelings.

Think about it: When you are struggling with feelings like depression or anxiety, you tend to talk it out. I know, because I have lived that reality personally. You want to talk to friends, you want to talk to family, you want to talk to your doctor, your hairdresser, your massage therapist, your neighbour, the person who serves you your coffee, the chat group on the net ... A psychologist just becomes the professional problem-listener. All of this talking, while possibly cathartic, only serves to embed you in the problem. These conversations become your cement boots at the bottom of that damn hole. Every time you talk it through, you are familiarising yourself with the likes of depression. Sadness becomes like an annoying neighbour who just keeps visiting.

Initially, when sadness came to visit, it brings home-baked muffins and a coy smile. You welcome it in because, of course, at that stage, it makes perfect sense that it should visit. Not only that, you instinctively recognise the fact that when any emotion comes to visit, it is prudent to honour it. You innately want to pay proper tribute to your sadness simply because it is wise to do so. Under these circumstances, all feelings are good. They are messengers and they are harbingers of insight, contemplation, and revelation. It is how the spirit whispers to you. You fellowship with sadness and commiserate together; you bond over mutual dilemmas. Sadness feels soothed and reassured. There was definite relief in bringing peace and acceptance to it.

But then sadness comes back the next day. Oh sure, there are more home-baked pastries, and it feels nice to be validated and legitimised again. You perform the same ritual—tea for you, coffee for sadness, exchange of pleasantries—and then *boom*, you launch into that sad, sad discussion. When sadness returns the next day, you innately know that a happy conversation is more in order. You are growing weary of sadness and want desperately to change the tone, but sadness just won't go there with you. After the next visit and the next and the next, the home-cooked treats just aren't worth it anymore. Sadness begins to feel more like an unwelcome intruder than a nice, friendly neighbour.

Across the many visits, you learn the life history of sadness, you become familiar with every eccentricity and personality quirk. You hear the same sad stories again and again and again until they are committed to memory. Now when sadness visits, you want to draw the curtains and turn off the lights, mute the television and silence the kids. You want to pretend you're not in, because sadness is so dogged and persistent. You laid out the welcome mat for a while and that felt right and good, but now it's just implied that there is a standing invitation, an open-door policy. Sadness feels comfortable to wander in at will, catching you unawares at the most inopportune times. Sadness acts like it owns the place.

It's usually at this stage that people seek my help, because now they are sincerely unsure whose house it truly is. Do I need to just give my house to sadness? Do I even have a right to kick it out? Should I keep the doors locked and pretend I've moved? People want to scream to their sadness, "Get the hell out of my house!" but they don't feel a sense of ownership within their own minds. They don't feel like they are the lord of the manor; they don't trust that they are the king of the castle.

When I speak with people about their sadness or anxiety or anger, they can very quickly and very easily tell me what depression sounds like in their mind, what anxiety feels like in their body, what triggers their anger. "Oh, I know sadness," they say. "I wish I didn't know sadness as well as I do, actually. I can tell you all about sad."

In the midst of this predicament, I joyfully encourage clients by telling them, "No, you don't have to vacate your own home for sadness." Their relief is palpable. "But," I continue, "you don't need to lock your door and barricade yourself against it either."

We are currently experiencing an epidemic of overly familiar negative emotions. These negative emotions can become bossy and pushy within the human mind, and they can't take the hint. This impasse is not resolved by slamming the door, essentially trying to keep negative emotions out. While this seems like the logical and intelligent thing to do, it is, in effect, merely barricading yourself against these emotions, armouring yourself against them. In my opinion, this is little more than a traditional medical or traditional psychological approach. The solution lies in making peace, not war.

"The next time sad visits you," I advise my clients, "lay out a delightful morning tea. Draw open the curtains and pull open the shutters. Set out biscuits and pastries and all manner of delicacies." You do not need to be concerned or trepidatious about a visit from sadness when happiness is seated at the table right next to you.

When somebody comes in feeling good, I tend to pounce on the opportunity to discuss the good feeling. I ask:

"So what does happy sound like in your mind?"

"What does excitement feel like in your body?"

"What triggers were there for contentment and peacefulness?"

By and large, the standard reply from clients is some variation of, "I don't know."

When I suggest that happiness is the remedy to sadness, when I point out that happiness is the antithesis of sadness, clients are simultaneously relieved and afraid. They are relieved because they instinctively know that this is true, and they are afraid because they have literally forgotten how to welcome happy.

We tend to overanalyse depression, anxiety, trauma, anger, stress, and other so-called negative emotions. Very rarely do we ever analyse happiness or contentment or hopefulness or excitement or passion, let alone overanalyse them. I would like to suggest to you that it is worth getting to know these feelings more intimately, because they can become more like strangers than best friends. I guarantee you that bliss and happiness and abundance and peacefulness want to be your friend. It just takes some deliberate effort to familiarise yourself with them, to become reacquainted. This is what children remember how to do.

CHAPTER 5

Anger Is Spiritual Guidance

Imagine that your emotional experience is like a staircase. Often you find yourself at the bottom of the staircase—down in the proverbial basement or cellar. The "dark," "low," "heavy" emotions are things like worthlessness, hopelessness, failure, and depression. I'm sure we are all in agreement that these feelings are horrible in the feeling and intrusive in the experience.

Now imagine that there is a landing at the top of the basement stairs. We could designate these middle emotions as "neutral" or "moderate" feelings – okay, average or indifferent. Let us take a few steps to the left, and here we come upon our final staircase. This one leads up to the top story. These are the "high," "light" feelings—ecstasy, passion, love, bliss, confidence, empowerment. We are all reaching for these peak emotional experiences, the highest heights, the widow's walk, as it were. (Unfortunate name, I know.)

Now, on a seemingly unrelated note, I want you to consider how you receive your spiritual guidance. Do you imagine that spiritual guidance comes to you as the heavens part and the angels descend? In other words, do you imagine that you'll recognise spiritual guidance for the unusual nature of it—you will awaken at night, perhaps, and see an angel at the foot of your bed? This is often the psychology of spirituality. There is a perception that in the spiritual basket are traits like meekness, subservience, sweetness, conviction, passion, wisdom, and the like. Embedded within this perception is the notion that some emotions fall outside of the spiritual basket. Actually, quite the opposite is true.

Let us go back to our psychological and spiritual associates and observe them through the lens of mastery. I don't think any sane adult is about to argue that children have perfected peace. They are not monks *om*-ing their way through their life experience. If we are to take them to be spiritual and psychological masters, it's fair to say that they aren't always meek, although they can absolutely be; they aren't always sweet, although they definitely have that in them; they aren't always passionate and wise, although they can certainly hit those notes. They feel and they feel big. They feel across the whole spectrum of emotion. They feel anger as well as peace, they feel disheartened as well as joyful, they feel unsure as well as certain.

Now, as we've discussed, in some regards slightly older children have been sullied by us crazy adults. We are not perfectly peaceful Tibetan monks either, and kids strongly and telepathically pick up on our hang-ups and eccentricities. They can sniff out, sense, intuit, and attune to disapproval even if it is wrapped in sweetness and light. They're spiritual masters, remember, people! Therefore, it is difficult to ascertain to what degree emotions like anger and sadness and fear would be typical for a child who was raised in an environment that was empowered and enlightened across the board—home, childcare, kindergarten, school, church, cafes, gyms. Until we reach this nirvana and find out, let us assume that emotions like anger, sadness, and worry have their place in the human condition. More to the point, kids move through their emotions—emotions like anger, for instance—better than their adult counterparts.

Let's pause the discussion here for a moment and go over a few assumptions I am going to be making. Premise 1: Because kids have not been kicking about in the human culture for as long as us, they are more spiritually and psychologically untarnished. I'm calling them spiritual and psychological masters. Premise 2: Kids get angry just like we do, for sure. Deduction: Anger must somehow be a component of spiritual and psychological mastery.

Let me see if I can explain it another way: God is love, right? To put it another way God is confidence, to say that another way, God is kindness, God is empowerment, God is passion. We often recognise that godly or spiritual people are the kind ones. We often expect that godly or spiritual people are the patient ones. We often assume that godly or spiritual people are the helpful, charitable ones—Mother Teresa, Jesus, the Dalai Lama, Gandhi. We take for granted that somehow God, or spirit, is present in helpfulness, charity, patience, and compassion—all very true, I'm sure you would agree.

God is synonymous with virtuous, positive feelings. However, God is also present in anger, in revenge, in bitterness, in frustration. Emotions, all emotions, are the angels at the foot of your bed. Emotions are the cherubim descending from the heavens. You literally receive spiritual guidance through your emotions, and it's all a matter of static.

As we have explored throughout this book already, we were raised in a thought-based culture. In Western society, intellect is considered superior. This is a largely tacit understanding, but it is nevertheless evident when you know what markers to look for. Intelligence has been historically esteemed across our culture. Now don't misunderstand, I'm not talking about academic intelligence here; we aren't talking about Einstein smart, although we do tend to hold traditional, academic intelligence in disproportionately high regard. I'm simply referring to every adult's ability to think something through—get to a doctor's appointment on time, schedule a bill payment online, resolve an issue at your child's school, or provide an account of the day's happenings in a coherent and logical way. Every facet of your experience is filtered through your intellect. Because of your enculturation, within your psyche, thoughts are given more credence.

To say it in a more interesting way, thoughts or "your head" are like the CEO of your personhood. If your selfhood was an allegorical corporation, your intellect or head would be the designated manager, the appointed oversight. This is because, within a culture that esteems thought, it makes sense that the thinking self would be seen as most competent. Don't just take my word for it—you can easily confirm this trend within your own life, when you reflect upon how many instances and in how many circumstances you are encouraged to, or expected to, be rational and practical and sensible and logical. The latter are all attributes of your head, your intellect. When you plan, you are using your intelligence; when you problem-solve, you are using your intellect; when you organise, when you explain, when you debate and justify—all intellect. These are all the stereotypic traits of a good CEO, a good manager.

Now, don't be confused, it isn't my intention to denigrate the intellect. Absolutely not. Your intellect is a massive contributor to your successful life. But because, from a very early age, it is taken for granted that the intellect is superior (or more competent at least), your head can become something of a tyrannical, stubborn despot within the figurative corporation that is you. Your head begins to take charge over any and all matters.

It's like there are departments within the "you" corporation. There is the thought department, there is the emotion department, there's the spiritual department, and the physical department. For most people, the thought department is revered, with the corner office and upper floors. There are hushed whispers or frantic hubbub when a decree comes down from the enigmatic top floor.

You may feel overwhelmed and think to yourself, for instance, *I'd love to just ditch work today and go spend time at the beach* or *I'd love to leave work early today and go to my kid's sporting event* or even *I'd love to just work my set hours today and leave on time for a change.* When this emotionally inspired impulse hits, what do you do? You know ... I know you know ... you *think* about it! You run it past head office, you send the request up to the bigwigs for formal approval. And what is the standard response? You know: "Denied—not practical!"

For many people, emotions have been demoted to the janitor's closet. Because of an insidious and profound cultural misunderstanding, we reduce our emotions to the mailroom level of personhood. Emotions are like the pimply, lanky sandwich boy; sure, he might eventually bring you something you want, but he's a hell of a nuisance all the same. Whenever the emotion manager is summoned to the top floor for a conference with the CEO—our ignoble thought manager—they might engage in a flaccid debate, but it's typically the

CEO who makes the final decision, ultimately holding the power of veto on all matters of import.

Within such a thought structure, with a CEO who wields ultimate power and control, there is often little self-analysis or self-critique of thoughts. "This is my organisation!" he booms. "I've gotten us to where we are today. I'm not about to let some young, inexperienced emotion manager start calling the shots." All this would be well and good if the CEO were able to collaborate within the organisation, lay aside his own agenda occasionally, or appreciate his own innate limitations. A CEO who is very smart but is lacking in humility or wisdom or balance can easily evolve into an autocrat.

For the majority of people, there are skerricks of self-analysis regarding their thoughts but often not enough for spiritual enlightenment or psychological empowerment. This is largely due to how trusted the internal CEO has become. This is all to say that Spirit, the Universe, your Inner Being, God, or Source has difficulty getting through to you via your thoughts. When you implicitly trust your own thoughts—your beliefs, your ideas, your opinions—there is a great deal of resistance to changing your mind. Just like our CEO, your thoughts regard themselves to be right. After all, they've been in charge for such a long time, and they've done a pretty good job thus far. When you form an opinion, you largely take for granted that it's a valid, legitimate, and correct opinion. You are more prone to mental rigidity than you'd like to admit, and many of your beliefs and opinions are rendered fixed and inflexible simply because it's what *you* think.

Imagine that into our figurative corporation wanders a third manager, Spirit. Let's say that the spirit manager wants to implement reform within the company. Let's say that spirit wants to overhaul the discrimination regimen within the corporation and implement a "love everyone" policy. Spirit is particularly interested in applying this new reform to the neighbouring company (a.k.a. your teenage daughter). There has been antagonism with the company next door because you have very different ideas about how to share the neighbourhood (a.k.a. the family home) appropriately. While your internal CEO and her internal CEO have had many conferences, these always devolve into idle threats and condescension on both sides. You become like two smart, slick lawyers pitted against each other, locked in a negotiation devoid of emotion or spirit.

If the spirit manager took a "love everyone" proposal directly to the CEO, it's likely that there would be some late-night deliberations. "I don't think I should be the one to be loving when she is being so judgmental," the thought manager might justify. "I don't see why it's always up to me to make the first move," the thought manager might reason. "You know, she has *always* been difficult, she has never respected me," the thought manager might explain. "I really, honestly think there is something wrong with her. She won't listen, she doesn't think, maybe its drugs," the thought manager might intellectualise. There is layer upon layer upon layer of thought—a tight, wadded-up ball of thoughts.

Under the circumstances, it would be extremely difficult for the spirit manager to make a case that is given a fair hearing. When given the "love everyone" pitch thoughts would begin to circle around specific objections as well as general ones. It's not just the case that, within your mind, it's considered foolhardy to love someone who is hostile. Conventional beliefs tell you that "it's dangerous to just love everybody; what if you're taken advantage of?" or "I don't know anybody who can just love everyone; I think that's a bit much, we're not all saints," or even "oh, I do love everyone … yes, yes I do … I do love her very much, but she's still a little bitch."

When you are entrenched in a particular stance—often completely oblivious to it or, worse, in denial—the spirit manager will not communicate with you through your thoughts. It's like there is static on the line and clear communication simply isn't possible. The spirit manager will approach you through your emotions. This channel of communication is much more pure and clear. The emotion manager and spirit manager work very well together. They have always been good colleagues, meeting at the water cooler to discuss their kids' soccer matches and their escalating mortgage interest. There is mutual respect and mutual understanding between them.

Now, with this in mind, let's jump back to the staircase we were discussing at the beginning of this chapter. Ah yes, our staircase, you had almost forgotten about that hadn't you. When you feel stuck in the basement of depression or fury or self-loathing, it can be difficult, nigh on impossible, to receive spiritual guidance through your thoughts. The very nature of something like depression is that it tends to dominate your mental landscape, like a twenty-four-hour looped tape. It's like the CEO is on a rampage about how every other corporation sucks and how everybody within your organisation is incompetent and spiteful. He wants to go on a firing spree and get rid of Sharon from emotions and Bob from spirit and Gill from physical. When the CEO is blinded by his own biases and presumption and insecurities and self-righteousness, it is like there is so much static on the line that hearing spiritual guidance within your own mind is tricky. It's just so busy and chaotic in there when fury or fear or hopelessness are swirling about. Even if a well-meaning person came to you and offered thoughts about your spiritual nature, your spiritual perfection, your worthiness—perhaps saying "you are lovable and loving," "you are perfection incarnate," "you are beautiful and delightful and spectacular"— if you were stuck in fury or depression or fear you would probably want to punch that person in the mouth, throw your coffee all over her, or stick his head in a toilet. You'd fire them or demand that they be escorted out of your building. In other words, you can't hear those sentiments when you are down in the basement.

The good news is, your emotions represent a much clearer channel for Source. While it can be chaotic in your mind and you have a hard time distinguishing one thought from another because of the barrage, you will not mistake strong emotions. You will not suppress or ignore rage, however much you might try. Depression will not go unnoticed, however much you might want it to. Worthlessness will not fly under your radar. These emotions *will* get your attention, if only because they are so deeply unpleasant that they shake you into alertness. It's like that classic scene from the movie where the protagonist flies into a rage or is consumed in a fervent rant and the trusty sidekick slaps him square across the cheek—the "pull it together, man!" moment.

Source-God uses this clearer line of communication—your emotions—to call you home, back up our figurative staircase. God is much smarter than people. What other people will often do, if they encounter you in depression, for instance, is try to happy you out of it. They may say well-intentioned but entirely unhelpful things like "other people have it worse," "you really should be grateful for what you've got," "it really isn't that bad," "it's time to move on now," or "you're making a big fuss over nothing." God-Source-Love does not try to call you from rage into happiness. That is like asking you to jump from the bottom step on your staircase all the way up to the top. It's like asking you to make an emotional quantum leap, and do you know what is likely to happen? If you feel the guilt of being angry or you feel the shame of being depressed, you'll try to make the leap for that person's sake and you'll catch your foot on the fifth step, smash your face, break your nose, and go tumbling right back down to the bottom—only now you are bruised and broken and feeling defeated as well as depressed.

Unfortunately, this is often what happens for people who are anxious or depressed. They attempt to get happy or 'do' happy because others expect and encourage it. They try earnestly to leap up many emotional steps at once and are, invariably, unsuccessful. We are very thought-oriented in our Western civilisation, remember, and emotions—from the head's perspective—should be solvable like a mathematical equation is solvable. There should be a workable, logical solution: if A + B = C, then "that person who is upsetting you" + "stay away from that person who's upsetting you" = "not being upset anymore." Simple, right?

Wrong. Emotions are not a science formula. When people attempt to make an emotional quantum leap from depressed to happy and the leap cannot be achieved, their emotional staircase is too broad and they risk tripping down further than where they began. They may feign happiness for other people's benefit or largely withdraw from people to be rid of the pressure, but failing to get happy layers guilt on top of the depression. People not only feel angry but guilty and angry. People not only feel anxious but ashamed and anxious.

Universe-Source-Love does not ask for quantum leaps but rather wants your emotional journey to be gradual and intuitive and manageable. If you watch kids, you will clearly see that they are masters of this process. When allowed to follow their inbuilt emotional guidance systems, their emotional GPS, they often reach for anger after feeling sadness. When left to their own instinct, there is no guilt or shame about the process.

When my children are arguing with each other—a common occurrence, I'll admit—there is this fascinating, noticeable pattern. My six-year-old son will be riling my four-year-old daughter up, and he might snatch a beloved toy from her. Her emotional reaction follows the process I've described to a T. She will initially become upset, and she may cry and call for my assistance. If I keep my distance and allow scope for a natural resolution, she will quickly, within a matter of minutes, swing to anger. She will chastise him and perhaps even retaliate. On some occasions, the situation will settle itself as she reclaims her toy, my son gives a final indignant expression, and they resume play with each other as thought the matter never happened. On other occasions, the situation will escalate as she attempts to reclaim her toy and my son does not concede. I may step in under these circumstances as a mediator.

My point is that kids, as the emotional beings that they are, can dance through their emotions because they allow a natural free flow. More importantly, they do not harbour guilt about this most instinctive process. As adults, we try to engineer artificial damns between our emotions. We try to assign them into mock categories of good and bad. We don't want to experience the bad emotions because they are designated bad. And if a hapless person were to stumble into the vicinity of a bad emotion, the unfortunate but logical response is to feel guilty or embarrassed or ashamed. Bastardisation of the terms *good* and *bad* serve no higher spiritual or psychological truth. As Shakespeare's Hamlet put it, "There is nothing either good or bad, but thinking makes it so."

God-Source-Love will call you from one step to the next one. Literally from one step to the very next one up. That's it. Just one gentle, easy, logical step up from where you are. From depressed into revenge. From revenge into anger. From anger into frustration. From frustration into stress. From stress into worry. From worry into indifference. Without judgement of the rightness or wrongness, goodness or badness of unpleasant emotions, the journey through them is not impeded by guilt or self-recrimination.

Haven't you noticed this? If you have been feeling depressed, there often comes a point at which you naturally and easily become angry. It probably happens a lot actually. This is because it's the next logical step. If you've been thinking how much life sucks, how you can't be bothered with it anymore, how it would be so much better if you weren't here anymore, those thoughts easily morph into thoughts about how you hate people, how irritating life can be, how stupid obligations are. There is often a yo-yo effect between depression and anger for a while. People can bounce from one step to the next, up and back, up and back, like some diabolical step class at the gym. But you may find yourself naturally moving into overwhelmed or anxious, and then you might notice a subtle shift into apathy or resignation, and then into indifference, and then finally into feeling okay.

When you have been stuck in depression and hopelessness, anger is the first logical step towards empowerment. At least when you're angry, you are asserting your opinion about something. You are stoking the fires and getting some passion back. Something matters to you again. By and large, society does not recognise that anger is a God-filled emotion as much as love and compassion are. The psychological reality is that you are only ever bouncing between two emotional points—I was on this step and now I've stepped up, or down, onto this one. You were depressed and now you're angry.

Because culturally anger has been given a very bad rap and is touted as a non-virtuous emotion, people who are depressed get stuck bouncing between two emotional points: depression and anger. *I was depressed and then I got angry ... then other people judged my anger as wrong ... so I felt guilty and I was knocked way down ... I was then spiritually guided back up to sadness and then anger ... and others condemned my anger ... and I fell back into depression ... I was naturally inspired back up to anger ... and I felt guilty for being angry ... and I fell down even further into guilt and humiliation.*

To use another analogy, anger is like being at base camp. On your ascent to the top of your emotional Everest, you need to stop first at base camp. Imagine if, when mountaineers reached the base camp, they were met by an angry mob taunting them: "I can't believe you're here!" "You shouldn't be here!" "Why aren't you higher up by now?" "You're so inappropriate, why are you here *again*!" "Get to the top already!" Now don't misunderstand; anger is *not* the peak of Everest. Nobody likes being angry, and nobody wants to camp there, especially children. But it is a necessary stop on the journey.

It is often *because* anger is misunderstood and damned that people find themselves stuck in anger and camping there. Spirit guides you with the intention of moving you through anger on the way to happiness, but when others discourage your anger, they can unwittingly circumvent your spiritual guidance. Of course, Spirit will very quickly and easily call people through anger into slightly more improved emotions, the next logical step up—overwhelmed or anxious, for example. God-Source-Love wants your journey to the summit to be smooth and intuitive.

When the spiritual and psychological masters do it, they make it look so simple. Indeed, they have made it look so effortless and so elegant that we oblivious adults remain largely ignorant. We dismiss as childish what we should revere as childlike. "Truly I tell you, unless you change and become like little children, you will never enter the kingdom of heaven" (Matthew 18:3). God does not want you to make an impossible leap and go tumbling back down the staircase. But love also wants the journey to be successful and empowering.

CHAPTER 6

Kids Don't Think Like You Do: The Psychological Power of Imagination

I was talking to a client recently about a health concern. He was a very fit and active man—he cycled, he rock-climbed, he swam. However, he had developed an unusual sensation in his face. Sometimes this sensation would foretell a migraine. He had dutifully seen doctors who referred to specialists who referred back to doctors who all proceeded to inform him about the various maladies that his mysterious sensation might denote.

One condition in particular had aroused my client's anxiety. It was a degenerative and incurable condition. The specialist had speculated that my client's jaw sensation was indicative of anything within the range of "nothing" to "terminal." (I know, helpful, right?) Now, nobody would blame my client for becoming anxious about this matter when a prognosis of "incurable" and "degenerative" loomed large above his head like a guillotine. But when I sat and spoke with him, I did not want to focus upon the medical condition. I wanted to focus upon the anxiety—and more specifically, the nature of the anxiety itself.

Now follow along with me here. Anxiety or fear is literally your own intellect turned against you. The experience of anxiety is very much a thinking problem—or more precisely, an overthinking problem. Remember our CEO from the last chapter? The CEO within your mind is the thought manager. It is the intellectual aspect of your personhood. It's quite simply your smarts. If the CEO within your mind got a memo about the office building being structurally unsound, you would say it's prudent for the CEO to take the memo seriously. You would say it's judicious for him to commission an engineer's report. You would probably say he's being conscientious to request a soil report.

But what if the CEO got a memo saying that the office building *might be* structurally compromised? Would it still be pragmatic to pay heed? What if the CEO got a memo saying that the office building was *probably secure* structurally? What if our symbolic CEO did not get a memo to say that the building was structurally stable, but the *absence* of such a memo made our CEO wonder if perhaps he should check it out, just to be safe?

Now I know we are stretching this metaphor as far as it will take us, but I guarantee that, at least in the case of the first two examples, many of you would say that he should absolutely respond to the memo and have the situation checked because … well … "what if?" What if he didn't act upon the information and the building started to fall down? What if he didn't act and the ground began to sink? What if he didn't act and people got hurt when the building started to fall down and the ground began to sink? Then what?

But what of our latter two examples? Do you think the CEO should check things out under the just-in-case conditions? I'm sure you've already surmised that the scenarios, as I've presented them, represent increasing levels of anxiety. Some may even go so far as to say that the fourth set-up (the "nothing-appears-wrong-but-maybe-we-should-double-check" scenario) seems more like paranoia.

The majority of people would respond to the first two situations and think themselves cautious. If I developed medical symptoms that concerned me, I'd be wise to check it out, wouldn't I? If I found out there was a leak in the plumbing at my house, I'd be foolish to not fix it. If I found out my children were not doing well academically, I'd want to get them some extra support. Makes sense! Within their own mind fewer individuals believe that they would respond in the third instance, in the "just in case" scenario. On paper they believe that they would be untroubled by the "just in case". But think a bit more about it. If I have insurance that will pay for an unexpected leak in my plumbing, it's all good, right? We are surrounded by examples of the "just in case". There are a plethora of times that our internal CEO will react, and sometimes react vehemently and strongly, to a "just in case" scenario. If I get the flu vaccination every winter to boost my immunity, then I won't catch the bug. If I have all the right baby supplements, and if I prepare all of my own baby food using organic produce, then my baby is sure to be fit and healthy. But what about the last example. The "nothing-is-actually-wrong-but-it-could-be" scenario. Few people would believe themselves to be fazed by this fourth circumstance, and they believe that they would comfortably offer no response.

But let me submit to you that your own internal CEO is often and regularly responding to very similar examples as the one given fourthly. You are just commonly unaware of this fact. You play the what-if game all the time—*all* the time. The rhetoric of the advertising industry is encapsulated in example four, as well as the pharmaceutical and psycho-pharmaceutical industries, media, fashion, cosmetics, finance, politics, the Internet … the list goes on and on. "Is your neighbour's dog carrying a deadly disease?" "Before it kills your children, watch this story tonight." "Do you think you will die one day? Here's a financial plan to help you manage the costs." "Could you have bowel cancer? Here's the screening test that will tell you." Your mind is constantly responding to a barrage of fictitious problems. The reason your mind gets so wrapped up in hypothetical problems, even problems that you know have a miniscule likelihood of eventuating, is because your imagination works in tandem with your intellect.

Your intellect tells you there is some truth to the supposed problem. It's true that I could have bowel cancer and not know it. It's true that I'm gonna die and a funeral will cost money. It's true that my neighbour's dog could be carrying diseases. It's true, it's true, it's true. Your intellect tells you that *truth* should be basis for your discernment. Even a skerrick of truth, even a hypothetical truth, even an imagined truth will demand your attention, and you will call it sensible.

Let's meander back to the client I was telling you about. His internal CEO had gotten a hold of a memo saying "Your building might be falling down" (in this case, "your body may be failing you and the facial sensation is just the first indicator"). His thought manager had responded with problem-solving and solution-finding. "What does this mean? How did this happen? What are the implications for my future? Could I have prevented this? How do I slow the deterioration?"

Initially, this solution-finding felt natural and helpful to my client. He followed a course that the vast majority of us would. He sought answers and clarification from doctors and specialists. Prudent, you would agree. But over time, he became embedded in the solution-finding and couldn't extract himself from it. Anxiety is often the word that we give to frantic overanalysis, hyper problem-solving, uber solution-finding. Your intellect will pounce on a perceived problem and become entangled within its own complicated and convoluted web.

You could consider anxiety to be synonymous with problem-solving, and you wouldn't be far wrong, but it's desperate problem-solving, it's frantic problem-solving. It's like an overprotective parent—helpful, but only to a point. "I'm here to take care of you, and my way of looking after you is making sure everything runs perfectly and everybody treats you perfectly and every experience is perfect and every outcome is perfect and every conceivable obstacle is avoided or resolved perfectly." So while doctors had presented my client with two possible outcomes, his mind had attached to the most serious problem and completely ignored the equally likely "lack of serious problem" possibility.

Your intelligence, your internal CEO, would consider it crazy to receive a potentially life-altering diagnosis and continue along merrily, assuming that it's probably no biggie. Your intelligence would consider it insane to be presented with this kind of situation and proceed happily, assuming that all is well. Granted, it is good to think about possible, future, theoretical outcomes and problem-solve from that basis. We humans are good at that, and it's served us very well. Taken on a purely thought level, you may thank an internal CEO for being fastidious and having good foresight. But remember that anxiety is your intellect working in consort with your imagination, and both are on hyperdrive. It is your imagination that actually gives the oomph to hypothetical scenarios.

This is why fearmongers like the advertising industry and pharmaceutical industry and fashion industry can influence you so strongly. Within your mind, you experience the convergence of three extremely powerful dynamics:

1. Your intellect leans in the direction of truth. If something even has the slightest potential of being true, then overlooking it is difficult to justify intellectually. It seems irresponsible or crazy within a thought-paradigm.
2. Specifically anxious thoughts masquerade as "help" initially, and then they have a way of morphing from protective to overprotective.
3. Your imagination sidles in from behind to bolster whatever (1) and (2) have got going on.

So now you don't just have a soundtrack of anxious thinking and frenetic problem-solving, you have a full movie in high-definition surround sound. Your imagination is tethered to your intellect, and this tandem assault is the essence of anxiety.

Our client friend was not just thinking "How did this happen?" He was playing a mental detective movie, courtesy of his imagination, screening memories of overexertion on his bike or discomfort on the computer chair or consumption of specific foods. Our friend was not just thinking "How will this impact my future?" He was playing a horror movie of an imagined future where he was a feeble invalid dependent upon his family. He was not just thinking "How will I cope with this?" He was playing a tragic movie of unfulfilled dreams and unrequited love—because, of course, his girlfriend wouldn't want to stay with him in his infirm state.

Into this very morose tale enter our heroes and heroines, the psychological and spiritual masters: kids. The fundamental and tremendous difference between child imagination and adult imagination is how fear-laden the latter typically is. As we have previously discussed at length, adults are accustomed to thought being the vindicator within the psyche. Thoughts hold remarkable sway within the adult mind when they are deemed practical, logical, and ultimately true. Adults don't appreciate that the splendour of childhood imagination is its unlimited and unfettered nature. Because children have not been marinating in the fear-based Western culture for long, they are able to access greater depths of happiness, invincibility, and personal freedom within—and because of—their imaginations.

Usually the extent to which their adult equivalents will let their imaginations soar to anything close to this extent is when they are sexually fantasising. Fantasy, play, and imagination are often relegated to this very specific and very narrow sliver of the adult experience, and in my opinion it does both sex and imagination a great disservice. Sex is often diminished in this sense, because fantasy and imagination are regarded by the intellect at childish rather than childlike. The knock-on effect is that sexual play and sexual fantasy are seen as infantile, illegitimate, and therefore shameful. Simultaneously, imagination is guilty by its association. Play, fantasy, and imagination are considered to be equally childish, and adults are expected to "put away childish things."

I believe that the pre-eminence of gaming represents a wonderful embracing of the psychological benefits of fantasy, play, and imagination—but that's a story for another time. Put simply, spiritual Truth still courses through the veins of young children. Divine Truth still rings in their ears. Human truth would suggest that, for all intents and purposes, any given individual is not likely to be a soccer player in the English premiere league. Human truth would suggest that it is not practical to try to make a career from art or music. Human truth would suggest that the odds of any one individual inventing the next global phenomenon are slim to none. Divine Truth, meanwhile, flies in the face of this human truth, and it's this Divine Truth that sets children free.

In Zen Buddhism, there is a concept of *beginner's mind* or *no mind*. In the I Ching, this sentiment is stated in similar terms, equating the mind with an empty rice bowl. *A Course in Miracles* describes it as "coming with empty hands unto God." In their play and imagination, children come close to this beginner's mind. They not only drop aspects of their own identities—transforming into mothers or police officers or pop stars—they can freely drop aspects of tangible, physical reality and mutate into mermaids, vampires, superheroes, or cats. The veil between physical and metaphysical realities is gossamer thin for children.

As logical and reasonable adults, we can be quick to discount children who say they commune with the birds or fellowship with fairies. Adults will titter amongst themselves with a condescending "aw, how cute," quite unaware that a child's expertise in play and imagination has literally become the door to the secret garden, the closet to Narnia. As children grow older, they can lose touch with some of this unbounded magic, but it remains in a more subdued form.

Kids often speak of themselves and think of themselves and, indeed, imagine themselves as noteworthy figures: brilliant inventors or heroic protectors, spectacular artists, or even powerful moguls. We adults, often psychologically inept and spiritually stunted, want to introduce a measure of logic to this unencumbered optimism. We want to bring a bit of reason to this wild invincibility, and we pronounce "That's nice, dear, but it's hard to invent something," "That's nice dear, but it can be dangerous to do that job," "That's nice, dear, but you may want a nice house one day, and that isn't a very good job if you want a nice house."

Seth, the discarnate entity given voice by Jane Roberts from 1963 to 1984, said, "You create your own reality." Abraham, the non-physical consciousness spoken by Esther Hicks, said, "You have come forth into this leading edge environment as powerful creators. You came forth to create reality, not regurgitate reality." Children want to instinctively harness their spiritual and emotional powers, and their imagination is wielded to creative ends, not anxious ones. But when we stifle their confidence in their own imagination, we smother their confidence in their creative power. They begin to think that perhaps their dreams of pop stardom are silly, they are wasting time trying to design a new contraption, or they aren't smart enough to be a surgeon or astronaut. They slowly and reluctantly conform to adult notions of possible and impossible. While the Technicolor of childhood fades to the dull, dreary black and white of adulthood, there is a nostalgia for those good old days when life was fun and exciting and full of possibilities.

While this may all seem esoteric and philosophical, the individuals, the adults, who have made monumental contributions to the world have retained this particular gem from their childhood. They squirrelled away the gem of imagination and fantasy into the furthest reaches of their own mind and refused to surrender it to the giants who went hunting for it. They retained confidence in their own ideas—their crackpot, outlandish, hare-brained, fantastical ideas. Iconic historical figures like Henry Ford or Leonardo da Vinci or Thomas Edison and more recently Bill Gates or Steve Jobs or Richard Branson put conviction behind their imagination. They concocted a potent brew of equal parts fantasy and courage—not a sour blend of imagination and logic—and amid the naysayers, look what they achieved. In the words of George Bernard Shaw, "Some men see things as they are and ask 'why?' Others dream things that never were and ask 'why not.'"

CHAPTER 7

Kids Know Their Own Value

Much of my work with individuals revolves around their sense of self-worth and value. As I'm sure you can understand, people struggling with depression or anxiety or trauma or anger do not necessarily have the most robust, positive self-image. But when I am working with parents, I notice that they too can be lacking in self-confidence and self-esteem. The issue of low self-confidence is not confined to individuals with mental health issues. It is a problem that runs rampant within the Western world. The flow-on effect is that adults frequently don't recognise healthy self-confidence and self-worth when it is in their midst, in their kids.

So let me put my hand on your forehead, place my thermometer under your tongue, and take your self-worth temperature. Let me give you your psychological physical and gauge how healthy your own self-esteem is. Because, you see, you can't teach what you don't know, and you can't be what you are not. So if you, yourself, don't have clear sight when it comes to this most foundational emotion—worthiness—then you risk misunderstanding it or misinterpreting it as laziness or complacency or irresponsibility or all manner of erroneous things when you witness it in your child. So let's get you up on the examination table and take a look.

As a parent, it is safe to say that you probably remember fondly the first time you held your precious child. Imagine the innocence of that newborn. Perhaps it is that one who is causing you so much grief now. We rightly regard infants as heart-achingly enchanting. Even some new parents are wary of holding infants or moving them too briskly for fear they will break. I remember feeling that way with my firstborn. Delicate, perfect babies are akin to priceless crystal vases.

Now let's play a little game and imagine that you literally owned a priceless crystal vase. First, think about the word *priceless* for a moment. That's more than a billion dollars, more than a trillion dollars. While you would, no doubt, be mindful to pour only the finest filtered water into your vase or delicately place it within a Fort Knox-ian cabinet so as to preserve its pristine condition, there are others who might not be so careful with your treasure, and there are more still who might seek to destroy and annihilate such a prize. But the magic of our vase lies in its nature: it is indestructible. While you would swear that a vase could be broken, smashed, or destroyed, in fact the miracle of our vase is that its beauty can only be hidden in plain sight.

Let's say that you didn't get to designate the most appropriate display cabinet for your vase. Let's pretend that it was completely at the discretion of others. Perhaps we could say that the priceless vase was a family heirloom, bequeathed to you by your great aunt but held in trust until your eighteenth birthday. Maybe distant relatives were assigned to keep it safe on your behalf. What if, out of sheer ignorance on their part, your crystal vase was filled with decaying, putrid, stagnant muck? It was never cleaned, and it was left to fester. Needless to say, it would be relegated to the farthest corner of the highest attic, as its bouquet singed the nose hairs of any hapless wanderer looking for the Christmas decorations box.

But its innate value could never be compromised, could it? What if, now being of age, you discovered that it was stashed away up there? Would you not scour and hunt for it? Of course you would. And it is my deepest wish for you that you remember this and take it into your heart: you were a priceless newborn once. You may have been entrusted to vase collectors who did not recognise you for your limitless worth. Perhaps they did not see it. Perhaps they did not know it. Perhaps they were expecting a shimmering crystal vase that refracted the light while it glistened on the window sill. Maybe they got a Ming vase and, being uneducated in the craftsmanship and artistry of such a masterpiece, they slapped in a can of Chum for Fido and placed it outside the back door, right next to the dog's water. But does a priceless vase lose its worth because it has been filled with mud and muck? Rot and rubbish? All it takes is a savvy treasure hunter to bring it back to its true glory.

Play along with my little game and do me the honour, à la *Antiques Roadshow*, of wildly and joyful proclaiming "Eureka!" We needed to scrub and pour and disinfect, but behold—what a treasure we have reclaimed. It is your essence. It is your Truth. You are worthy beyond description; you are precious beyond measure.

If you have ever looked into your children's eyes and seen how invaluable and irreplaceable they were, you know the utter perfection of the human being. You have merely forgotten what you once knew for yourself. Parenthood can be a magnificent window into the heart of the Universe-Source-Love, because as you love your precious child, so too does the Universe-God love you. The overwhelming love you have for you children is literally you feeling You loving. When love comes full circle in this way, parents can begin to better understand their own value. See yourself as you see your own child rather than how your parents saw you. Then you will have a better chance of including yourself in this most auspicious category of "utterly perfect."

You see, when you understand your self-worth, when you've found your own empowerment, you are not as likely to mislabel it in others. You can better appreciate natural confidence and comfortable self-worth when you observe it. Moreover, you are not unnerved when other people are still walking their own worthiness path and are not yet as far along as you are. You look back upon them with love and certainty, knowing they will inevitably join you but not worried that they aren't there yet. Parents typically have an advantage when reclaiming their own self-worth exactly because of their children. Ironic, I know—you may be at odds with your child, you may be embattled with your tween, you might be at war with you teenager, but get ready, because your enemy is about to become your saviour.

In those early days when you were enraptured by your new bundle of joy, you understood something incredibly profound but entirely contradictory to the Western mindset. Your newborn was simultaneously the most cherished thing you'd ever been fortunate enough to hold and also the most useless thing you'd ever know in your life. Let me elaborate. One of the most anxiety-making and esteem-sapping phenomena in the developed world is the adult obsession with productivity and achievement. These criteria are touted as the pillars of an industrialised country, but they are corrosive to psychological health. Before notions of achievement and productivity were introduced into your psyche, you did not have any problems with self-esteem. It does not occur to children, especially young children, that they will be assessed on the basis of achievement. Consequently, they are not striving to achieve in conventional terms.

In our culture, we straightjacket our sense of worthiness by binding it to values like accomplishment and output—action-based values. Children very quickly get the message that it is what you do that matters. "Did you *do* your best? Did you *work* hard? Did you *try*? Give it a *go*. Give it your best shot. Get out there and do it. Make it happen." There is nothing inherently wrong with these sentiments, but they are indicative of how action-laden our modern vernacular is. The person who offers the most action or the best action or even some action is revered.

As the importance of achievement filters through to deep levels of the psyche, it mutates. It is not just about action, it is about culturally approved action. Children very quickly learn the societal standards around achievement and, through psychological osmosis, pick up on subtle messages about what is worth achieving and what is not. While of course there are individual differences, generally speaking a Western culture considers intellectual achievement to be primary; running a close second is achievement within the sporting arena (physical achievement). Academic intelligence and physical prowess were clearly assets for our ancestors, but they are overvalued within our modern society like relics from another age.

Creative achievements, emotional achievements, and spiritual achievements in particular are minimised at best or ignored at worst. Since children come into this world hardwired and ready for hook-up to the emotional and spiritual aspects of the human experience, they require firm training to orient them away from this natural compass. They are graded against peers, praised for standardised work, and disciplined for deviance.

Speaking of deviance, within psychology there is a lot of scientific methodology because, as you will recall, psychology has its origins in the medical-scientific model. Psychology is especially enamoured with statistical analysis, and you will not find more rigorous statisticians than psychologists. My aptitude for statistical analysis is rudimentary at best, but let me see if I can make my point in this way. There is this thing called the bell curve: it is a graph that essentially looks like a bell, and it represents the distribution of a data set. Just imagine in your mind a little hill, a little Jack and Jill hill. They went up their hill to the well (the top of the bell shape), and Jack came tumbling down the other side. Many sets of data within psychology conform to a bell-shaped curve. In simple terms, this means that the majority fall within the middle of the bell and the minority fall around the rim of the bell. To say it another way, the majority make up the hill part while a small minority make up the ground levels.

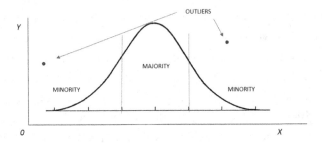

Within any set of data, whether it's the distribution of Year 4 student grades in a class or the distribution of alcohol consumption on weeknights, the majority will fall around the average. By definition, that is what makes something average—the majority hangs out there. So if we take our Year 4 students as an example, most of them will get Bs and Cs, while a few will get As (higher than average) and a few will get Ds and Fs (lower than average). I know, I know, "get to the point already" yes I see you are getting bored with this math stuff. The point I'm getting to is that within the vast majority of bell-shaped graphs, there are outliers. Outliers are like statistical anomalies. They are the rogue data. One child in our fictitious Year 4 class may do genius-level work and perform exceptionally above the average while one child may be chronically struggling and perform atypically below the average.

And what do statisticians do with these fiendish data figures, you may ask? They eliminate them. Yes literally. In order to establish an average, in order to mathematically and with raw data establish a standard when it comes to psychological trends, the vast majority of figures are fudged. They're tweaked. They're doctored. Not a lot, I'll grant you. But the point I'm making is that at the most basic level of science, we are erasing individuality. We can't include rambunctious little Suzie's genius-level grades because she will drag up the mean (the average).

I know it seems harmless to just eliminate little Suzie from our nice graph because we *mostly* have our bell shape. It *mostly* conforms to our expectations, so what is the harm in modifying one little score? By the time children are being scored and tested, they are measured against an established, entrenched, codified standard. If little Suzie is the most spiritually savvy and psychologically masterful student in the room, science is happy to designate her as atypical. She's an irregularity. While the majority settle into the norm, the perspicacity of little Suzie is written off.

I hear you, "big deal" you say. I can see you rolling your eyes. Yes, once is no big deal; sure, a handful of times isn't a problem; but at a systemic level, this is how average is maintained and how we end up believing that it is psychologically good to be normal and typical. We don't seize upon the individuality and confidence of little Suzie and study how and why one child can excel beyond the average. We don't say to ourselves, "Uniqueness is natural, individuality is normal, if one child can be so powerful and extraordinary let's assume that all children have the same latent abilities. How might we unlock the extraordinary and expand upon it? How could we make extraordinary more ordinary?"

When we have mechanisms, albeit suspect mechanisms, to quantify and reinforce normal, this idea permeates deeply within mass consciousness, and achievement—standardised achievement—is the order of the day. When you mix action-based values like productivity and accomplishment with a cultural bias towards the intellectual, you get a recipe for comparison. Ultimately, it's this comparison that's the poison in the stomach of worthiness, and once it has taken effect, it cause paralysis of authenticity, individuality, and confidence.

Adults become expert compare-o-metres. We compare the output of what *we* do with the output of what *they* do. The trusty statistician in our heads is ever present to remind us to "stay normal" in the process: look normal, speak normal, eat normal, move normal, and produce normal things. A child with a talent for art or music or empathy or listening or prayer or visions is not necessarily discouraged outright but is equally not encouraged outright. When children are themselves, when they *be* emotional or they *be* spiritual or they *be* creative, they are equally, and in fact more naturally, aligned with God-Source-Love.

It does not occur to young children that they will be evaluated. Full Stop. Let alone evaluated on the basis of certain aspects of their personhood above others. They do not compare, and they do not expect comparison. With a free spirit, they wear clothes that they want to wear. They say what comes to mind with joyful abandon. They draw and dance and sing "like no one is watching." As adults, we first need to console ourselves that no one is watching before we will be bold enough to be this authentic and unique. But hell, watch out ... if someone *is* watching ... whoa ... back to normal you go! Adults who have acclimated to a comparison culture can be burdened with an overactive internal statistician. This anxiety-making, depression-provoking, rage-rousing inner critic will work to slay confidence and self-worth.

For many years now, I have offered my clients this analogy to explain the inner critic aspect of the adult psyche. Now remember, evaluation and comparison in themselves can be extremely useful; this is a unique human trait that has allowed our species to flourish. However. evaluations and comparisons prime us to judge, and we do it to the hilt. This omnipresent judge judges you, your partner, your friends, strangers, celebrities, situations, organisations—everything, really.

Imagine that within your mind there is a courtroom. You sit as the judge, complete with black gown and white wig, and you preside over the court from your perch. Within spiritual traditions, this vantage point would be synonymous with your Spirit; within Eastern traditions, this vantage point is regarded as the observing self; within psychoanalysis, this vantage point is thought of as the superego. It is the job of a judge to judge, needless to say, but on what basis do you make your judgements? On what evidence are you basing your ruling?

Imagine that in this courtroom there are two desks: one for the prosecution and one for the defence. Now let's pretend that we have bill number 2497—the matter of your worthiness. From the back of the room, a little devil makes his way down the aisle. This smarmy, slick creature clip-clops as each cloven hoof meets the marble floor, because of course in my imagination our little devil is the mythic Baphomet (the goat-headed man). The diabolical brute pulls a little red wagon behind him, and let's add a squeaky wheel just for effect. Teetering precariously within the pint-sized wagon are volumes of leather-bound books. The little devil makes his way to the prosecutor's desk and begins to unload volume upon volume onto the desk, generating deep thuds that echo around the room and reverberate out through the hallowed halls. The judge sits in wait.

The little devil, adjusting his spectacles, begins to rap his gnarled and yellowed fingernails, like eagle's talons, against the desk. The door at the back of the room gently and tentatively swings open and in flutters a little angel. She floats above the ground with a sheepish, apologetic grin and quickly settles herself at the desk for the defence. Before making herself comfortable in the chair—which is hard to do with those cumbersome wings—she reaches behind to her shoulder blade where she pulls out a crumpled old piece of paper from some mysterious hidden compartment between her feathers. She is startled as the judge, wielding the hefty gavel, brings it down with a bang and declares, "Court is now in session."

The little devil within your mind is ruthless. He presents to the judge reams of evidence against your worthiness. He lives up to his title, and he prosecutes with precision and malevolence. His arguments are slick and fast and convincing. "Exhibit A," he announces as he waves one of the leather-bound volumes above his head, holding it aloft for dramatic effect. "Kindergarten ... remember when you asked that stupid question and the other kids laughed?"

"Exhibit B ... at six years old, remember when you didn't study for that test and lied about it when Mum asked why you failed?"

"Exhibit C ... at ten years old, nobody wanted to dance with you at that birthday party."

"At eighteen, you had sex with that guy even though you didn't really like him that much."

"Exhibit H: at twenty-two ... at thirty-two ... Exhibit Q: at thirty-four ... at ... at ... remember ... that time ..."

Reaching a crescendo, the little devil pronounces with unerring conviction, "Stupid! Liar! Idiot! Ugly! Slut! ... I rest my case, your honour." Every volume has been cited, page upon page of mistakes and wrongdoings and guilty pleasures and missteps and bad judgements and regrettable moments. The assault is brutal, but the final decision ultimately rests with the judge. There may yet be hope.

The little angel rises from her seat, accidentally pitching her chair into the aisle and knocking over her glass of water. It turns out angels are clumsy when earthbound. Her voice quivers as she reads from the tatty piece of solitary paper. "Um ... well ... there was that time at age eleven when we helped the neighbour's dog."

"Objection, your honour," the little devil rebuts smugly. "Dad didn't want us going near that dog."

"Sustained," bellows the judge.

The little angel gropes around for some semblance of confidence. "Oh ... well ... we are liked by many ... well, some people. We're friendly, we're kind ... um ... ah ... that's all, your honour," and with a lump in her throat she whispers, "I rest my case."

Within your own mind, your own defence is often so lacking in conviction that any judge with even a modicum of common sense is left to regrettably conclude, "Guilty as charged ... I hereby deem you worthless!"

The adult mind has an endless ability to evaluate. Good boy! Bad girl! You failure! Stupid idiot! What a moron! When the little devil has become cocky, he will launch appeal after appeal and deliver subpoena after subpoena whenever some minor or major infraction passes over his desk—anything to take it to court and win the case. This is how worthiness is eroded over time. It is subtle and insidious and would do any evil genius proud. This is why notions of "devil" and "evil" exist within the collective consciousness in the first place. We have personified the dualism of our own psyche to mythic proportions.

But, as always, we adults have it backwards. The impotence of the little angel is an illusion. The vast majority of adults may *feel* like the little angel is out to lunch, but in reality her power is so monumental, so epic, that there can be no comparison. For young children, the balance tips in the little angel's favour every time. They innately understand that they are lovable and loving. "You're so pretty, Mummy. I'm pretty too, aren't I?" they chirp. "I can run faster than all the other boys in my class. I can run around the oval four hundred times, Mum. I can run to infinity," they boast. If we did not train our kids out of their natural state of worthiness, we would not, as adults, need to undo this programming from our childhood in order to make our way back to this quintessential Truth.

It is here that your magnificent child comes in to save the day. Within your mind, you might have experienced the barrage of the little devil for so long that it's hard to remember what the little angel even sounds like. But any parent can recall, even if the memories seem distant, what it was like in those first precious days. You knew the perfection and lovability of your infant. You beheld your baby with awe and reverence. Then your child began to scream and cry and poop and some of the lustre went away, perhaps, but you were still able to clearly see their radiance. You cooed, you babbled, you kissed, and you smiled. Parents are often able to open themselves to their own kindness and compassion through the gateway of their child.

Especially during their child's infancy, parents can access previously untapped depths of patience and kindness. It is so paradoxical to the Western mindset that the things we prize most highly, our babies, are also the most useless, but it speaks to the spiritual Truth that worthiness has never, and is never, based upon action. You didn't think about how dependent your baby was; the child could literally *do* nothing, yet he or she was miraculously and simultaneously *be*-ing everything. You didn't demand, "Get up and walk, you little dummy." You didn't think about how unproductive your baby was and insist, "Just learn this eating thing already, you're so useless." You didn't think about how inept and reliant your child was and complain, "Another bath, really? You need another bath? You can't even do the simplest things." When you are flowing love to your infant, who elicits it with a flash of doe-eyes and dimpled cheeks, you have met at the level of Spirit.

We ask very little of an infant. We are happy to be depended upon, and babies unapologetically surrender to dependency. Within this cocoon we glimpse the power of pure worthiness: "I deserve to have my every need tended to. I expect good things to flow to me effortlessly and easily. I will lie here and accomplish absolutely nothing. I will achieve zip, I will undertake zilch, I will complete nada (well, maybe I'll succeed at a little vomit and a burp), but you will dote upon me and adore me nonetheless." You can glimpse the power of aspects of the Sacred Mother, the Divine Feminine—she is patient and compassionate and gentle and wise. She is love incarnate.

Now fast forward to today. Your child may have lost some of that secure worthiness, some of their natural confidence, some of that pure well-being. But you may have equally lost some of your own. Don't fall into the trap of thinking yourself the master of life teaching the new student how to make a way here on this place called Earth. Tap back into that Divine Feminine. (Yes, you too, dads, we aren't talking *female* here, we are talking *feminine*. Men can do the feminine as much as women can do the masculine. It's just yin and yang). Tap back into that Sacred Mother and draw upon your wisdom and insight. Be humble! Let humility flow back into your parenting and bathe you in the revelation that the student is the master and the master is the student.

Oh what a glorious spiritual dance it is. Children will teach you how to surrender to your innate worthiness because they are not striving to achieve and they are not clambering to perform. Don't be quick to dismiss this proclivity as laziness or naivety or childishness.

CHAPTER 8

Children Live in the Now:
Evading and Lying and Denial, "Oh My"

Allow me to set the stage before I launch into this chapter, because in order to acquire the skills of the master you need to first lay the foundations of the apprentice. If you can first understand how your psychology works at a basic level, you can understand why evasion and lying and denial are often psychologically healthy, especially as they relate to your powerful now.

Have you ever met one of those people who will bring down the emotional tone of an entire room, someone who is chronically pessimistic? We say that these people are like a black cloud rolling in, or they came in like thunder. Think about the psychological insights that come from these kinds of commonplace idioms. We take for granted that, on an action level, a person entering a room "under a black cloud" will mope about and sulk. Such people will offer boring or cynical conversation, their body language will probably be closed or slumped, and their tone of voice may be low or monotone. On an action level, this is all noticeable to everybody, and it is obvious that one person's pessimism can have a ripple effect throughout the room.

Some may feel stuck in conversation with a melancholic person and offer furtive eye-rolling to bystanders. Some may gravitate away from a morose person, deliberately avoiding conversation or politely and quickly disengaging from a conversation if they have accidentally stumbled into one. A few may band together and surreptitiously excuse themselves to gossip about the offending buzzkill. This action journey is well understood by the majority. A depressing person arrives at a party, and people respond to the depressing person by moving away or disengaging.

At a somewhat deeper level, there is a parallel emotional journey going on. There are still many who appreciate an emotional undercurrent, but some fail to appreciate how powerfully it contributes to the psychological story. Within the common vernacular, we speak to this undercurrent by trying to capture the essence of it, saying things like "that person has a bad vibe" or is "flat" or "a downer." Within mass consciousness, it is a given that one person's emotional tone can impact upon others and "bring people down." A person arrives at a party and is clearly in a depressed mood, and people respond by harmonising with this depressed person like catching a contagious cold. Somebody with a powerful emotional set-point, positive or negative, can be like an emotional dominatrix and can set the tone for an entire room.

But as with the common cold, some rare and fortunate individuals seem to have the natural antibodies to ward off those germs even if it's spreading through a room like wildfire. Some individuals who are stable in their own emotional tone will not easily succumb and can remain peppy and positive. At the deepest level, there is a parallel spiritual journey. The essence of the spiritual journey is that you draw to yourself the experiences that have the potential to serve you the most. You are powerful and magnanimous, and you literally create the experiences that you expect to have. In our everyday lingo, we say something was a "self-fulfilling prophesy," or karma or we ponder the "lesson" or "journey." of something.

People with a depressed mood will literally create a depressing experience for themselves. This process is understood by an enlightened minority, but the majority are so used to looking at things through the lens of action, or to a lesser extent emotion, that the spiritual can easily go unnoticed. It makes perfect sense once you understand how to look at it, so let's borrow the action and emotional elements in order to elucidate the spiritual.

If you are a person caught in anger or depression, you might receive a party invitation and think things like, "Oh no, I can't be bothered to go to this," "I hate parties, I feel so awkward, I never know what to say," "People don't talk to me anyway, I think they've invited me because they feel sorry for me," "I don't think anyone I like will be there," "Why should I have to do this sort of stuff anyway?" or "Argh, people are so stupid." This handful of thoughts paints a very clear picture of the mental landscape of this person. If a person's psychology is predominantly tinged with this depressing hue, it's easy for most to see why he or she would be feeling depressed about parties, well about everything really.

Now, if such people have a change of mind and decide to venture out to the party, they may be feeling hopeful ("It will be okay"), or they may be feeling obligated ("I probably should make an appearance"), or they may be feeling guilty ("I've missed so many parties already, I'm a terrible friend"). Even with a change of heart, it is likely that the dominant attitude of this party-hating individual will be one of indignation, or anxiety, or misery. If you can appreciate, at least intellectually, that this emotion can be felt by others upon their arrival, you can understand why people who expect to have a miserable time will create a miserable time for themselves.

Any person who walks into a room bearing a morose demeanour is figuratively "felt up" by others energetically. Your Spirit sizes up the other person's Spirit and gives an energetic once-over. You "feel their vibe." They receive a cheeky brush-up of their emotional privates. In the same way that people will hide their literal unmentionables from prying eyes, they also try to hide their emotions from peeping psychics. But while you may be able to cover yourself physically, you cannot cover your emotional self.

You see, every person is psychic. We all attune to the emotions of others, regardless of whether it is done consciously or unconsciously. When people "vibe" with others in a positive way, we call it charisma or the "it" factor. People who have harnessed a good degree of emotional authenticity and confidence are influential. Their power of influence has less to do with physical qualities like what they say or where they go or how they look. It is predominantly their emotional set-point;

it's how well they have harnessed their power, and this power is of the Spirit. The fact that very few understand this quality to be emotional prowess, energetic attractiveness, or more specifically spiritual power speaks to our naivety. But while many may not understand the nature of such enigmatic power, almost everyone can recognise its existence through personal experience.

Surely you've noticed when you've been at parties that there is a natural gravitational pull around some individuals while the opposite is true for others. Some people will fade into the background, becoming almost invisible, so they can move about in a clandestine manner. Others will draw a crowd and carry conversations effortlessly. If you can accept that this emotional reality is as much a reality as the physical reality, and if you can allow for the possibility that there is more going on in a crowd than physical bodies moving about, then you have travelled some distance on the journey to understanding your child or tween or teenager.

Some people are labouring under the illusion that it's the haute couture clothing you drape upon your physical body or the delectable appetisers that you serve for your physical taste buds or the cologne that you splash on your physique or any number of material factors that account for success or likeability or happiness. While it is certainly true that things of the material world are sublime and beautiful, it is the emotional undercurrent that adds the lion's share when it comes to somebody's "presence" in a crowded room. A happy person will have a happy time at a party, and while it would be accurate to say that it is because of psychic/spiritual factors, that notion freaks many people out. It is just as accurate to say that it's because of knowable, perceptible emotional factors, and this is a ship that many more people are comfortable to board.

We have a cultural aversion to psychic phenomena because such things have been relegated to the paranormal corners of society. Every adult to a varying degree, on a spiritual level, is telepathic. The extraordinary, hippy-dippy, woo-woo connotations of this wording sends logical, sensible types into a tailspin. Society at large would much prefer these ethereal abilities were confined to occult factions like astrologers or numerologists or clairvoyants or tarotists or (when

I was growing up) goths or emos. Well, heck, for some people, occult factions would even be naturopaths or aromatherapists. But, in reality, we are all utilising our psychic abilities constantly because we are all using our emotional abilities constantly.

When you get a feel for somebody, when you get a bad vibe, or likewise when you get a good vibe, you are picking up on non-physical information, and this is psychic. Every husband knows when he has committed some kind of transgression in his wife's eyes or in his daughter's opinion or in his husband's assessment. He knows that he is wandering into a minefield to say, "Are you okay?" If he receives a reply of, "Yes, that's okay [daddy/dearest husband of mine], it didn't really matter that much," he is wise to strap on his combat helmet, hit the deck, and wait for the shrapnel to start flying. In other words, even the most logical, intellectual, thought-oriented person knows full well when there is an energy mismatch. Even the biggest dunce knows when somebody says one thing but means another, especially when it's an intimate partner or close relative.

This is the telepathy that exists between us. True, some people have more refined abilities than others, but it is an aspect of our innate spirituality. So while it's often true that actions speak louder than words, it's also true that emotion (energy) shouts. While I say to secular clients that their children are little emotional barometers, I would say to spiritual clients that their children retain psychic abilities long into their physical life experience. Some lose their awareness of it as they acclimate to dense, physical, logical society. Some never lose it but learn to disregard it as unacceptable or weird. Some preserve it but have an on-again off-again relationship with it. Some harness it and hone it and own it.

Now, I hear you ponder, why have we taken this detour? I want you to see if you can get a sense of how masterful children are in their psychology. They make choices that are very different from their adult counterparts, and they hold opinions that are juxtaposed to their adult peers. In order to bring it all into sharper focus, it is helpful to make a direct comparison with what we adults are inclined to do as their equivalents. Adults will play this action, thought-oriented game with each other; children not so much.

For instance, I attended a party last night, and I found myself in a conversation with a couple. The conversation had started because I was discussing something with the hostess, and the couple, who'd been on the periphery at the beginning, had positioned themselves within the conversational space. You know what I mean—within earshot of the discussion in such a way that it would be rude to exclude them completely, but not exactly close enough to count them as active participants. Then comes that telepathic knowing. Sensing that there is somebody on the verge, and the necessary minor adjustments are made by the group collectively to bring them into the fold. The hostess was suddenly called away to tend to one of the kids who'd broken a glass outside. And now the three of us were standing in silence, and for a few beats it was an awkward silence. I'm sure you've experienced that sensation before too. Your spider-sense starts tingling and you telepathically know that somebody wants to exit the situation pronto. I just imagined that there were subtitles reading *Awkward Pause*.

Now I am highly adept at reading body language and facial expression as well as reading energy (or emotion) because I do it in my work every day, so there is very little that somebody can get past my awareness. Hence in this type of scenario, I am at an unfair advantage. I forged ahead for the sake of politeness, and I attempted to engage this couple in casual conversation, hoping to put them at ease. But I think I failed miserably. With each question I offered, such as, "So where do you work?" I received a perfunctory response: "A few towns over" (arms folded, body angled away, tight smile). The subtitles read: *Oh no, now I'm stuck talking to this person.*

I made another valiant effort, knowing that I was probably pushing a rock uphill. "So how long have you been living in this area?"

With eyes diverted, one partner made reference to the other, "Oh I don't know, how long would you say?" (Subtitles: *Help! You carry this conversation for a bit.*)

I offered one last effort. "Do you have children?"

"Ah, yes, they're around here somewhere," came the reply. (Subtitles: *Oh please stop talking to me, stop talking to me, stop talking to me.*)

And then the sweet relief as I suggested "I think I'll go check on my kids and make sure they're not getting up to mischief."

As I broke away from the situation I imagined the subtitles might read: *Oh thank goodness. I think it's time for us to go now.* And indeed, they did soon after that.

Now I know from my understanding of psychology that there was certainly no malice intended by this couple. They were possibly anxious about banal conversation just like I often am. I don't believe their demeanour had anything to do with me personally, so I did not take it personally. But it makes me smile to think how such a scene might have played out with children. As adults, we play this game of social nicety. It makes me question, are we really fooling each other, or do we just pretend that we are? I believe we are much more intuitive than we give ourselves credit for. I believe our telepathic and clairsentient abilities are much more active than we'd like to admit.

With that said, I'd like to play the scene back in my head and remove the pretence. If I had been bold enough to do what all of us were feeling, I might have not uttered a word, turned my back, and walked away. If I'd been brazen enough to say what all of us felt, I might have said, "Well, this is an awkward moment. I think I'll go and save us all some trouble." Kids don't play the game like adults do. Their rules are entirely different, and their game is arguably more fun.

Children are very good at allowing revelations to flow, and they make their "Now" moment as fun and as easy and as happy and as authentic as it can be. Where adults get bogged down in thoughts and conventions and other people's opinions and logical reality, children are lighter, more playful, more inspired, and more ingenious. In their powerful Now, kids are better selective sifters of their reality—a reality that is more fluid and fluctuating than adults like to believe. Adults are of the opinion that reality is reality, and you are being evasive or dishonest if you take liberties with the truth of now. Younger children will use their powerful Now to patch together a quilted reality that is more pleasing and more satisfying. They are stitching at the level of emotion and spirit and less so at the level of the physical. They will give an account that, for all intents and purposes, is sheer fiction at the physical level, but it is psychologically healthier.

As you sit there aghast, let me clarify what I mean. First let's remember that, for children, physical reality is not held in such high regard. They do not feel hindered by physical, factual, actual reality because they intuit the deep and powerful, emotional and spiritual levels. Let's also remember that children instinctively know that emotion makes the greatest contribution to the Now—said differently, kids want to make Now as emotionally good as it can be. So to recap: kids don't feel obliged to tell it like it is because they prefer to tell it like they want it to be; but even more than that, kids prefer to feel it like they want it to be.

I was speaking with two parents regarding their young son recently (yes, I know, I speak with many parents regarding their sons). Last year at school, their son had "fallen"—their word—into a friendship with an unsavoury character. These lovely parents had formed the opinion that their young monsieur was impressionable and had been led astray by this child scoundrel. They had taken the old adage of "falling in with the wrong crowd" quite literally and sought my help in empowering their son to making better choices. In detailing the problem to me, they made note of some burgeoning yet uncharacteristic traits in their son, such as lying and denial and evasion.

As I do with all parents, I assured them that I would wave my magic wand and make all things better ... okay, only joking. I certainly assured these delightful and well-meaning parents that their son was magnificent, albeit misunderstood. They emphatically agreed with my assessment. I explained that my agenda was to improve his self-esteem and restore his self-confidence. They championed this agenda as vehemently as I. But what I often do not tell parents at the first meeting is that I will probably side with their son on many more occasions than with them. This is usually not what parents expect to hear from a psychologist, so I try to save them the shock—at least until our third meeting.

After meeting with the parents, I was then introduced to their son. He was utterly delightful. He spoke with the annunciation of a young Laurence Olivier, and when he flashed his eyes, they had the charm and innocence of a young James Dean. When I asked him why he thought he was seeing me, his reply came swiftly: "Because the naughty boys want me to hang around with them." And there it was! In one fell swoop, he had created psychological distance between himself and the naughty boys and aligned with his mother's rhetoric about victimisation. Those naughty boys enticed and tempted and goaded him into naughty behaviour, and now he was caught in their naughty trap, so when he was being naughty, it was completely out of his control. Curse those naughty boys!

My young client was caught between a psychological rock and a hard place. He wanted to play with whomever he chose—and let's face it, the naughty boys are often up for the most fun—but he was made to feel bad because these naughty boys were wrong. What possible resolution is there for a young man who just wants to play with whomever is most fun on the day, who doesn't want to talk to a stranger about a non-existent problem (by his estimation), who just wants to get back to living happily ever after? Lie! Ignore! Evade! Deny!

Of course the solution is to lie. Why would you *not* lie? Of course the solution is to become evasive and deny and just say what you know people want to hear. Why would you not? What ten-year-old is going to say to a parent or a teacher or a principal or a psychologist, in any given moment, when they'd just like to be playing and relaxing outside, "Well, if you really must know, I played with little Johnny because he's the most fun, and I was just thinking about having fun that day, and then you said I couldn't play with him, and that made him seem like even more fun. It was fun to stir you up, sir; it was fun to rile you up, Mrs. Longbottom; it was fun to stick it to little Suzie. I hate to break it to you, but I *am* one of the 'naughty' kids sometimes, Mum." But since young boys don't have the nous to articulate their own psychological brilliance, the best that they can do is gauge what people want to hear.

Children begin to stab around in the dark for explanations or justifications that will hopefully please their parents. It is utter nonsense for an adult to pose a loaded question that essentially amounts to "Why have you done this thing that I don't like/don't want/ don't approve of?" and await a satisfying answer. If the young mystic replies, "Because I think it's okay," he is disapproved of and disagreed with; if he replies, "Somebody made me do it," he is reprimanded for denial; if he replies, "The dog did it," he is reproved for lying; if he replies, "I don't know," he is pounced upon for evasiveness and asked to think again. The sum and total of this psychological tussle is an admission of guilt: "Yes, Mummy, Daddy, I did that thing that you don't like. I'm sorry."

"Now that's better. Doesn't it feel better to tell the truth? You know I don't like that thing, don't you?" We harp on it for a bit: "I don't know how many times I've told you about that. It just seems to go in one ear and out the other with you." All the while, you can watch the child's spark and spirit drain away.

Our ideas of good parenting can be so backwards. While the intellectual battle has been won, the emotional victims lie dead and dying on the ground. Guilt has gained ground within a psychology that was previously fortified against it. Children, being emotional barometers, learn quickly what will please a parent or teacher. They so desperately want their powerful Now to be as happy as possible that they will placate an adult—particularly an adult they love—with false promises or white lies or outright fabrications as they secretly think to themselves, *Just drop it already.* When they know what response an adult wants, they will either appease and become disingenuous or hold firm, become stubborn, and stick to their story.

Let's talk about the master evaders, the Jedis of denial, the samurai of the lie. Teenagers are experts at this psychological duck and weave. I was speaking to a seventeen-year-old client recently who had been dabbling in online pornography since puberty. He found it enticing and thrilling and risqué. He was explaining his dilemma to me in much the same way as my younger client had. "It's inappropriate," he confessed.

Now, I'm always suspicious when I hear adult phrasing coming from the mouths of babes (not that he was a babe anymore). This type of terminology is not something he had come to of his own accord, because children will not hint towards self-deprecating comments unless they have picked it up from others. Granted, this client was not so much a boy as a young man, and he'd had many years out in the world learning how to effect self-deprecation. When I met him the entrenched guilt was obvious.

I also had the privilege of briefly meeting this young man's father, and he was a charming gentleman in every sense of the word. He was a sturdy, imposing figure with a jovial, warm presence—think Santa Claus. By his son's account, this father was supportive and well-meaning. And yet, even with an obviously kind-hearted and understanding father, this young man found himself guilt-ridden because his actions were ostensibly wrong and inappropriate.

This father, as is usually the case, was taking a punitive approach to my client's actions and would confiscate technology as a remedy. But over many years, this approach had proven itself to be nothing more than a temporary fix. Once the technology was returned, it wouldn't be long before my client was tempted back into his online antics. The ineffective stalemate that this father and son had arrived at could be consolidated into a thrust-and-parry joust:

"Stop doing that thing you enjoy!"

"I don't want to stop doing that thing I enjoy."

"But I disapprove of that thing you enjoy!"

"Okay, I'll try to stop doing that thing I enjoy to make you happy ... but it turns out that my willpower isn't strong enough to stop."

"Well, just stop doing that thing you enjoy!"

"But I don't know if I want to stop doing that thing that I enjoy."

"But I disapprove of that thing you enjoy!"

"Okay, I'll try ..."

And around and around we go. Particularly when it comes to teenage children, parents' sense of possession and dominion is challenged, and rightly so. It's as if parents are emotionally scuttling alongside their teenager as their teen is walking his or her own path. In a coach-like manner, parents will dash a few paces ahead trying to clear the path up of debris or obstacles, almost shouting at their child, "Going good, honey, doing well there, darling, watch out now, watch out, watch *out*! See there, you almost tripped over that log, just be very careful, we don't want you to trip now do we, careful, *careful*! Oh, good thing I saw that before you tripped, let me move this out of your way." Parents can be like traffic controllers waving their fluorescent batons, trying to guide their teenager to a safe landing into adulthood.

Conversely, some parents can be like drill sergeants, jogging behind their teenagers and essentially yelling, "Look where you're going, you ass wipe! Look where you're going! I said look where ... oh great, now you see, you *see*? I told you to *look*! Yeah, you've tripped and hurt yourself, haven't you, yeah, you're hurt? Well tough titties, princess. I warned you. I warned you, didn't I? Now get up, *get up*! Well, maybe you'll listen better next time."

As these young men and women negotiate their way through their own lives, they want to scream, "Will you just leave me alone! Get off my path! This is my path, get back onto your own path. You're not helping me." In order to stake a claim to their spiritual and psychological independence, children—particularly teenagers—will lie and evade and deny. When it's a choice between guilt and indifference, any psychologically savvy person will opt for indifference. Teenagers will feign concern, ignore reprimands, and offer perfunctory explanations and cursory justifications. When you feel guilty about your choices— about the things you genuinely want and desire, about the person you are becoming - you have wandered into hopeless and helpless emotional territory, you are in a psychological wasteland, and it's a good place to avoid when you can and however you can.

Now I can appreciate that all of this may be a little hard for parents to accept. Trust me, I speak with parents and children and teenagers all the time. I know the psychological hurdles that need to be jumped in order for such a bizarre concept to even resemble sense for many people. Parents have very legitimate objections, and I can understand their rationale. While it all seems to belie every notion we have about good parenting, I'd like to explain why, at the deepest level, reworking your *now* moment is pure brilliance.

Remember from back at the beginning of this chapter that your psychology doesn't just impact upon your Now moment at an action level. Your psychology sets the tone for what you expect to happen. A sullen, gloomy person expects sullen, gloomy things, while a happy, cheerful person expects happy, cheerful things—not all the time, obviously, but enough of the time that it becomes an emotional trend. The tone of your psychology impacts upon your attitudes and beliefs about what the world is like, what other people are like, and what self is like. Your psychology is imbued with the power of Spirit, because you are Spirit first and foremost; you are heir to the Universe itself. Your thoughts are powerful—very, very powerful—as you would expect from a child of God. Your thoughts are powerful enough to create the situation you expect to encounter.

If you're miserable, you expect to encounter misery, because everything you think is filtered through a lens of misery. Hence, you are likely to encounter misery; people will respond to your misery because they can sense it and they don't like it. Your mind is so phenomenally powerful as to create—not through action, although that is the farthest outworking of your mind, and not through emotion, although that is an outcropping of your mind too obviously, but through thought, the very genesis of creation. If thoughts are imbued with the power of Source, and if you are standing in your powerful Now—a moment that is fresh and new unto the Universe, a born-again moment, a moment where your humanity converges with your spirituality—does it make sense to you that, when you have reverence for the power of Now in union with the power of thought, you are less inclined to squander that powerful moment?

Young children especially want to wipe the slate clean in every powerful Now moment, and because they are less encumbered by the bigness or the heaviness or the seriousness of the past or the future, their task is made easier. Kids will take poetic license with the truth because they unconsciously understand that the truth as it appears in physical terms is not ultimate Truth. So to say that children, particularly young children, are lying is not necessarily accurate. Tweens sure, teenagers absolutely, but the younger they are, the less accurate this construct becomes.

Where does a selective memory stop and denial begin? Surely this is a subjective judgement. If your playful, exuberant puppy tracked mud through the house on Sunday morning and you growled at him, sending him plodding outside in disgrace, would you say that your puppy was in denial if he came bounding up to you on Sunday afternoon looking for a walk and a belly rub? It may be the case that *you* haven't recuperated from the thirty minutes of soapy water and hard scrubbing, but that's simply because you are not the psychological master that you could be.

As we move along the age scale, I'll concede that older children will fabricate and lie and evade. Ultimately, the mastery of it is telling it like you want it to be, not necessarily how it is. If you can accept that your psychology is powerful, therefore your thoughts are powerful, and by extension your words are powerful, it makes sense to tell a happier story—not because it's more accurate, not because it's what literally took place in the past, not because other's will agree, but because in a powerful Now moment you get to make your story whatever you want it to be.

As Abraham-Hicks puts it "you cannot have a happy ending to a sad story". You just cannot. As adults, we want to fixate on the unhappy details, on the issues and problems, on the "what's wrong" of life. Consequently, many adults tell a very sad story indeed. The story is not inaccurate or invalid, it's just depressing, it's a depressing and anxious story. The pages are filled with the tragedy of existence and lamentations about injustice and suffering—chapter after chapter. But children live in the knowledge that "happily ever after" is always coming. Just borrow a few of their pages and take a few of your cues from these budding authors. Give yourself permission to edit out some bits that don't serve you. Give yourself license to splash around some fiction. Make your powerful Now a happy comedy even if yesterday was an Orwellian tragedy. Kids will!

CHAPTER 9

Taking the Easier Road: If It Doesn't Serve Me, I Don't Wanna Do It!

I was speaking with one of my longer-term clients about her son recently. I have so much fondness for this family; they are so lovely and wonderful and sincere. Their young son, who is nine years old, was on the verge of expulsion from school because of his antagonistic and aggressive behaviour. I had been thinking about this young man for the days preceding our appointment. He is so full of fire and strength and conviction, and yet he is completely lost as to how to wield his strength. I imagine him like He-man.

For those who don't know, *He-man* was a children's cartoon series in the eighties featuring a muscular, Herculean protagonist. My brothers and I would watch it before they were subjected to the "girlie" She-ra (the female equivalent). At the end of the catchy He-man theme tune, there would be a scene where He-man held his massive sword aloft victoriously as lightning bolts shot from the blade. I envisaged my client's aggressive young son as a hero who couldn't control his own sword—like Arthur trying to extract Excalibur from the stone or Thor trying to lift his colossal hammer. Epic heroes who have not yet acquired the strength or wisdom to wield their own power are dangerous.

From the beginning of my work with them, this mother and son had been locked in an argument about who should feed the dog. Mum believed that chores are an obligatory part of life, while her son was of the opinion that he didn't purchase the dog and therefore he shouldn't be held responsible for feeding it. You can easily see the validity of both perspectives when you look at it objectively. However, of most interest to me as the three of us wove our way through the conversation was that Mum represented a more traditional perspective while her son was articulating, albeit clumsily and vaguely, a more contemporary opinion.

Mum held strongly to the tenet that "life is hard" and "life sucks" and "you just need to suck it up and do hard, unwanted stuff." She even went so far as to verbalise this with statements like "I have to do things I don't like," "If I have to do it, you do too," "I guess I'll just have to do it if nobody else will," and "If I don't do it, it won't get done." This is a very prevalent belief system amongst adults, particularly women. On the flipside, her young son was expressing the very elegant principal, "I don't want to do what I don't want to do."

You may be tempted at this point in our discussion to shoot off half-cocked, "How ridiculous, Deidre, you can't suggest that people should just do *whatever* they want *whenever* they want! That's the stupidest thing I've ever heard! Nothing would ever get done if we lived in that la-la land!" But while you may scoff, I would like to redirect us back to the spiritual and psychological masters. This young man went on to profess that if the laundry light was kept on—that is, if it wasn't so dark in the laundry at night—he might find it easier to get the chore done. He also explained that if the tin wasn't so high up—if he didn't need to climb onto the washing machine in order to reach the shelves—that would also make the job easier.

You see, children are not monsters. They are not little devils (adults are more like that). Children want to be helpful, they want to be kind and considerate, they want to uplift others. Why would a true spiritual and psychological master be other than that? Children also want to be independent and resourceful and responsible. But in a culture that directs you away from your natural proclivities, in a society that directs you away from your natural compass, you end up in a tailspin thinking that north is south and east is west. We covertly teach our children that tough is noble and easy is "slacking off." These children grow into adults who believe that pleasure is bad and abstinence is good. Easy is bad and hard is good. While people still harbour strong, secret desires for pleasure and fun and ease, they are taught that these pursuits are not virtuous.

In truth, hard is just hard, no matter how you spin it. Pleasure and ease are natural—and that is why, no matter how hard we may try societally, we cannot prevent people from following pleasure-seeking impulses like sex, drugs, food, and shopping. Trying to quash these natural instincts means they go underground and often play out in destructive ways. But it is not because sex or drugs or food or shopping are wrong in themselves, but because sex + wrong = guilt, drugs + evil = guilt, food + bad = guilt. Guilt-ridden individuals are defensive and angry and unmotivated and depressed and stressed and unwise. The drugs, the food, and the sex are red herrings; it's predominantly the guilt that births problematic drug-taking, its chiefly guilt that births problematic sex, it is mainly guilt that gives birth to problematic eating.

Now, our young man's father was much like the father we met in the first chapter. He was a traditional authoritarian through and through, and he took a punitive approach to fatherhood. "Toughen up, princess," was his mantra, and many in our culture would agree that a *job* should not be made easier or more fun but a *person* should become more steely and resolute. Fortunately for our young man, his mother was beautifully wise and powerfully compassionate. She appreciated, at least in theory, the virtue of self-care and self-kindness and self-protection. Because this mother had access to insight and contemplation, she was able to understand where her son was coming from. But when I asked her if she could respect his position, she offered a resounding no.

"Why?" I inquired.

"Because if I have to do it, he does too."

Isn't it fascinating that our young man did not wish to feed the dog because he thought it was unfair to require something of him that he had no interest in. And ironically, this was exactly the argument his mother was offering in her defence. She thought it was unfair to require something of her that she had no interest in. "I don't want to do the dishes, I don't want to clean the house, I don't want to cook the meals," she complained. (FYI—nine times out of ten, the people who are causing you the most problems are the perfect mirror for you. They are either reflecting your own issue back to you or they have the antidote to your issue.)

The difference between our mother and son was that she wouldn't give herself permission to take the antidote that her son offered— which was a lovely pill of ease. Our mother felt burdened by the hard work of family life. She drew upon determination to meet these obligations, and it was making her miserable. By contrast, her son did not feel burdened by obligations. He would perform the tasks he wanted to, and he would minimise the tasks he did not want to do. He was more able to orient towards fun and ease and could therefore better maintain relaxation and contentment. At times, given the sometimes hostile home environment, even he could only find apathy or indifference, but that was still relatively better than guilt or hopelessness.

At this point in our conversation, the mother began to resign to her inevitable fate as the house slave. "So I guess I'll just feed the dog then." I pointed out to her that she did not have to surrender into a victim mentality in the hope of a fast resolution, to which she retorted, "Yeah, but I can't control what he does, can I."

"Exactly!" I said emphatically, pouncing on her accidental insight. She said it with a tone of defeat, whereas I wanted her to realise that we were in fact on the cusp of imminent empowerment. "That's exactly right!" I proclaimed. When you cease efforts to control another person and focus that attention on yourself, you have stepped into your own power. Children demonstrate this to us all the time, if we have the discernment to notice it.

This woman was a font of wisdom. She was a kindness oracle; she was a loving sage. She definitely had it in her to recognise what was previously going unnoticed. Her son was better able to find himself in ease and indifference, but he was no Gandhi, he was no Buddha, he was no Muhammed. A young, smug, foolish, pimply Arty trying to yank Excalibur from the stone is not the great King Arthur … yet. But when *she* was owning her power in the household, she became the cornerstone. She was the mystic, she was the goddess, she was the white witch. Or, as *A Course in Miracles* puts it, the miracle worker within any relationship is simply "whoever is saner at the time," and in this family, the prestigious title would be hers. It was often not her son's (although he could accidentally stumble upon some insights of his own) and it was usually not her husband's (although he held wisdom in his own right).

So I asked our mother, "What if you did things the way your son does? What if you cared less? How would that actually look?" When her son cares less, he sometimes doesn't feed the dog. Rather than responding with nagging and badgering, I asked her what *she* would be inclined to do if she took a leaf from this book. Taking everybody else out of the equation, ignoring everybody else's opinions, disregarding everybody else's desires, what would she do?

Initially she found this concept very confronting, as most adults do, because the polite police in their mind begin to blow the whistle and throw around charges like rude, selfish, and mean. She was finding it hard to limber up her mind in order to make this 180-degree pivot. She was rigid in her initial forbearance. "I'd just feed the dog, I guess."

"But do *you* care about the dog enough to *want to* feed it?" I asked.

Taking a leaf out of her son's book, she gave a blatantly honest answer: "No."

"So what would happen if you didn't feed the dog?" I inquired, knowing full well the answer.

"The dog probably wouldn't get fed—not regularly, anyway."

"And are you okay with that?" I persisted, much to her chagrin.

"Well, no, of course not."

I continued, testing her patience. "So if he doesn't really care, at least not enough to feed the dog regularly; and you don't really care either; and if he won't feed the dog out of obligation and you don't want to feed the dog out of obligation either, why not just get rid of the dog?"

And then the protests began. I'm sure you can anticipate them as easily as I could.

"Oh, but he really loves the dog!"

"We don't want to get rid of our dog!"

"That seems cruel to the dog."

And here we had come perfectly full circle.

Kids are masterful at taking the <u>easier</u> path. They are not looking to take the easy path; rather, they naturally orient towards the easier of two. *Easier* is a relative term. Kids are exceptionally good at subconsciously ascertaining the path of least resistance. Adults have this natural ability also and are often equally adept at ascertaining the path of least resistance, but adults are impeded by rhetoric about easy being bad. So while they may know full well which path they would prefer, they will choose the hard one but hate and resent it. When kids find themselves at this fork in the road, they take the path signed easier because they are not psychologically encumbered the way adults are.

Remember, as we have explored regarding anger, sometimes you are choosing between two difficult alternatives. When you are selecting between the hard step or the less hard step, kids will try to stand on the less hard one if they are given scope to follow their own guidance. Consider the following chart:

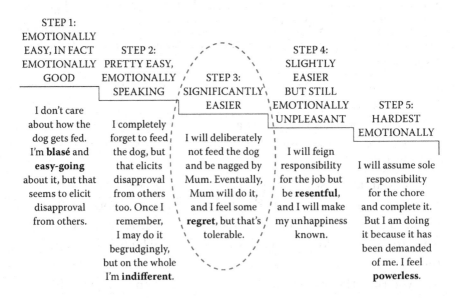

STEP 1: EMOTIONALLY EASY, IN FACT EMOTIONALLY GOOD

I don't care about how the dog gets fed. I'm **blasé** and **easy-going** about it, but that seems to elicit disapproval from others.

STEP 2: PRETTY EASY, EMOTIONALLY SPEAKING

I completely forget to feed the dog, but that elicits disapproval from others too. Once I remember, I may do it begrudgingly, but on the whole I'm **indifferent.**

STEP 3: SIGNIFICANTLY EASIER

I will deliberately not feed the dog and be nagged by Mum. Eventually, Mum will do it, and I feel some **regret**, but that's tolerable.

STEP 4: SLIGHTLY EASIER BUT STILL EMOTIONALLY UNPLEASANT

I will feign responsibility for the job but be **resentful**, and I will make my unhappiness known.

STEP 5: HARDEST EMOTIONALLY

I will assume sole responsibility for the chore and complete it. But I am doing it because it has been demanded of me. I feel **powerless.**

My young client would find himself psychologically and emotionally drawn to Step 3. At times, he would vacillate between 2 and 4, but he was mostly hanging out on the third step. I hope that it is clear from the diagram that parents will often try to coach kids towards effort and difficulty, whereas kids are inclined to move in the opposite direction.

If our mother took her cue from her psychologically savvy son and gave herself permission to walk the easier path, she could have gotten rid of the dog. But wait—would that have been the easier path for *her*? Probably not, because as much as she resented feeding that dog, she also loved that dog. If she allowed herself to walk an easier path, she might have found peace in feeding the dog herself but deliberately decided to do it solely for her own reasons. Would that have represented an easier path for her? Definitely, but she might have needed to work hard to find peace from her current set-point of powerlessness and resentment.

My suggestion was that she might send the dog on a pseudo-holiday and inform her son that the dog has gone on a vacation, given that nobody wanted to take responsibility for its basic care. You see, in her nagging and prodding of her son, our mother was holding *herself* in disempowerment. She was achieving little else than that. She was attempting to control his behaviour with bribery or pleading or guilt or anger or threats and failing. Therefore, she was feeling ineffective, resentful, and unkind. The two of them were just meeting up in Craps-Ville and hanging around there together. The more she begged, the more he resisted; the more she demanded, the more he resented; the more she took over, the more he disengaged. Which is all to say that both of them felt disempowered in their interactions with each other. The respective manifestation of disempowerment differed—a little begging for her, a little resentment for him—but at its most basic level, it was all a case of "same guy, different hat."

Disempowering yourself in order to meet others in their disempowerment is like abseiling down from the summit of a mountain. Imagine you are standing atop a high mountain peak. It is so high it's snow-capped, and you can see spreading before you a glorious expansive vista. Imagine that this is the height of your emotional experience: joy, rapture, happiness, maybe bliss and exhilaration. You couldn't be more high. At the very bottom of this mountain is a swamp. You can only just see the treetops of the swampland below you from the vantage point of the apex. In the swamp it is dark, musty, and smelly. Here are the lows of your emotions: sadness, fear, worthlessness, hopelessness, anger. They are swampy indeed.

What if one person in a relationship is blissfully standing atop the mountain and the other person is stuck at the bottom bellowing, "I'm down here in this swamp! Come down here and get me out! I want to be up there with you! Bring me up there!" It could be a spouse, it could be your child … or maybe it's you stuck in that dank swamp pleading for rescue. If you notice another person is stuck in sadness, or mired in condemnation, or fixed in judgement, or lost in anger, going down to meet them in the swamp is a futile exercise. Why? Because now you are *both* stuck in the mud!

You know what I'm talking about. Our mother thought it would be helpful to convince her strong-minded, strong-willed son that he should relinquish his hard-won independence for a cause he didn't care about. Fat chance! Equally, my young client made valiant attempts to try to negotiate his mother out of her position. Not a snowball's chance! People will try to convince each other out of anger; they will try to debate with each other about the inaccuracies of their respective judgments; they will try to negotiate with a clearly biased agenda. And what happens? Both parties end up defensive.

If you descend from your mountain peak, from your happiness and clarity and insight, in order to meet somebody in the swamplands of misery and confusion and anger, you might hope you can haul them up. "Tie this around your waist!" you yell as you throw out your guide rope. The person might proceed to tie it around and then hang loose and limp, a dead weight at the end of your rope. You work hard to pull the both of you up. You make the effort, you strain, you are determined. Meanwhile, your loved one relaxes, watching the scenery pass by, offering very little effort of their own, enjoying your hoop-jumping as you strain to help him or her feel better, maybe not noticing the life draining from you over the hours and hours of gruelling, unrelenting physical torture.

You eventually gasp with your final breaths, "Why aren't you helping me? You have to put some effort into this climb too."

"Oh no, I can't," comes the feeble reply. "I bumped my foot back there, and now my sock is bothering me, and someone needs to think about dinner anyway. You're doing a good job. I don't want to take over. I wouldn't know how to anyway."

Perhaps you foolishly believed you had enough pep and stamina for the both of you. Perhaps you wanted to be kind and helpful because after all, you *are* kind and helpful. Maybe you expected them to reciprocate at some point. Maybe you just thought you could change somebody. But all the while, it's *you* who becomes exasperated. You have given them their daily fish but they never learned how to catch their own.

Our beautiful mother and son were often mired in the swamplands together. Under these conditions, it is far more likely that children will disengage, ignore, walk away, and distract. They will find a slightly better feeling. They will reach for their grappling hook, cut the line that is tethered to you, and begin to work hard on their own ascent, leaving their beloved parent behind if necessary. They will emotionally turn on a dime and climb like a mountain goat up their own emotional scale, leaving parents eating their snow, so to speak.

Kids intuitively understand the spiritual and psychological truth that if one person can stay joyful, if one of you can hold on to happiness, if there is one who can stand firm in acceptance, if someone can reach for wisdom and clarity—or to put it another way, if someone can remain loving even while another person is harsh, miserable, foolish, or condemning—then there is still hope. If you, as a parent to your beloved child, can hold fast to the understanding that it's your clarity that helps another, it's your confidence that finds solutions, and it's your happiness that eases the situation, now you have everything to offer as a parent.

Our mother was disallowing natural consequences to flow from our young man's choices. She was trying to protect him from the obvious result of his choices. She was trying to do the thinking for him. She was trying to recognise the consequence for him. She was trying to guess what would be best for him and drag him to it. She was essentially trying to protect him from the results of his choices. Ironically he was taking an easier path, and as much as she resented it, she still tried to make it yet easier. When he was making a foolish choice, she would return like for like. But when you are seeking to protect another person (like our "yes" mother from the beginning of the book), when you are seeking to make your child's life easy, when you are trying to smooth your child's ride, you do not see your child as powerful. You do not imagine them to be resourceful and resilient and capable.

Allowing this young man to live through some of the natural aftermath of his choices, albeit a muted aftermath, would leave him better equipped to determine his own easier path for himself. His teacher is Life, which is another way of saying that his teacher is Love, which is another way of saying that his teacher is Spirit, which is another way of saying that his teacher is God/Source. A strong-willed, strong-minded, heroic young man like my client wants to live life on his own terms. He needs to bumble and fumble through things often. As he learns to wield his mighty sword, he may even do himself an injury sometimes, but he is up for that challenge. He was birthed into this life eager for the thrill of that, even if his parents were not.

When his mother attempted to assume the mantle of teacher, she was stepping in where she did not belong, and she actually interfered with the curriculum as God/Source would have it. It's like her son passed his test paper out of the nearest open window, and she tried to cheat him into an A grade. In one breath, she would say she abhorred the easy road, but in the next, she would try to cheat him out of his own Life experiences. When you appreciate that the headmaster/mistress is God, why would you ever step in and try to take over the lesson?

If Mum could find her own empowerment, if she could keep her eyes on her own assignment, if she could focus on her own climb, and make her way to her own emotional pinnacle, the vista would sprawl out before her. She would regain access to her own resolve and clarity and inspiration. Her lesson was self-care—maintaining healthy psychological detachment, releasing guilt, and ignoring another's agenda, all things that her son was much better able to do. His lesson was in discernment—bringing balance to things, articulating an opinion in a powerful persuasive way, and finding the best choice among various options. While his empowerment was in the realm of the masculine hero, albeit a juvenile hero, her empowerment was in the realm of the feminine sorceress.

Learning to respect what my young client was saying for the epiphany that it was—"I just don't want to do what I don't want to do, unless it's easier and more fun"—gave this straightjacketed mother permission to do the same. But it did not mean that she substituted his opinion for her own. While her son had mastered childlike things, he could equally find himself bogged down in childish things. While our mother had forgotten the art of childlike, she was often more astute and had certainly put away childish.

In summary, psychological and spiritual masters are not looking for easy, but they do recognise the subtle but profound difference between *easy* and *easier*. When they are given the latitude to learn from their own life experiences, children can easily recognise that it's easier to take five minutes to feed a dog than to lose the dog altogether. It's easier to get a homework assignment completed than to go to school poised for a fight or wracked with guilt. It's easier to be friendly than to wander the schoolyard with nobody to play with. You know as well as I do that it feels wonderful to achieve, but it's achievement borne of personal inspiration and personal motivation that is thrilling. That's the gold of life. It's satisfying and fun. Achievement borne of obligation is leaden and heavy; it's demotivating and effortful.

So if the dog went away, giving our young hero a visceral, high-definition, surround-sound experience, he would probably feel discomfort, and he would be more empowered to revise his choice. Do a boring task but have the benefit of a loving dog, or don't do a boring task and find another family to care for the dog. Either way, the dog wins.

CHAPTER 10

Selfish versus Self-full: I Am the Center of My Own Universe

*S*elfish is such an interesting and loaded word. There is such psychological depth to it. In our culture, we have determined that selfishness is not a virtue, and to a point it isn't. But think about the antithesis of selfish: *self-less-ness*. This is often considered a virtue amongst adults. We use it synonymously with *nice* or *giving* or *helpful* or *saintly*. The word *selfish* is thrown around like a grenade or cracked like a whip. It is levelled at people we don't like or used as self-criticism or self-damnation. Often it simply becomes a tool in the toolbox of conformity. But in order to even decide whether someone is being selfish, or not, you literally have to be self-ish in the judgement of it.

I was speaking to a client recently about her casual sexual partner. She was feeling great frustration towards him and couldn't isolate what the frustration was about. On the one hand, she knew that she enjoyed the sexual aspect of their relationship, and she knew that she enjoyed being desired. There was passion and connection and fun between them. On the other hand, she perceived the relationship as temporary, and her logic and pragmatism was telling her that temporary wasn't a good foundation for her relationships.

She amplified this judgement within her own mind by citing the fact that her partner was in an open relationship with another woman as well as having additional sexual partners beyond that. Moreover, she had recently requested that communication between the two of them cease, and he had ostensibly honoured this request for a week before reinitiating text-message contact under the guise of seeking clarification. My client found this extremely disrespectful, and she felt it unfair that he was not upholding his end of the bargain.

While stuck in the discomfort of this internal conflict, she was uncomfortably judgemental. She was uncomfortable about her own recognised judgements. She was labelling him as a game-player, as suspect, as greedy, and as selfish. Her level of self-awareness and psychological mindedness was very good, and she saw that it was as much frustration with herself, being drawn to a relationship that ostensibly had no future, as it was with him, the cad that he was. It was when she used a particular descriptor that our discussion became most interesting, and we began to shift her perspective and allow for deeper insight.

She deemed him to be egotistical. She had determined that he was egocentric, and she was levelling the accusation as a moral judgement in much the same way that most do. He was somehow ethically bankrupt because he was operating through his ego in discernible, unapologetic ways. I would suggest to you that the term *ego* has been bastardised by popular culture and pseudo-psychological ideas. It is used in the common vernacular as an insult, just like the term *narcissism* (but don't get me started on that one). These terms have been adopted in our recent history and are highly reflective of our psychologically minded culture. However, I believe that within our modern society, this phraseology remains tantamount to the selfish slur, just a more highbrow, sophisticated version. It is just the thinking (wo)man's insult.

When you understand that ego quintessentially means your sense of your 'self', you can more easily appreciate that a person literally cannot be without ego any more than he or she can be without self-hood. Your ego is like the human filter through which your Spirit flows. Your ego is the channel through which your consciousness flows. So it is not that somebody should be self-less, although that psychological myth still permeates mass consciousness. It is more accurate to say that adults mandate each other to do ego in a polite way. To say it differently, do ego in a subtle way or in a subversive way. And indeed, this is what the majority of adults do.

In our example, my client held the erroneous belief that she herself was not egotistical. She was not selfish, because she wasn't obvious about it. She was so expert at stealth-selfishness that it was even flying below her own radar. You see, you can only look at or judge another person's behaviour through the lens of self. You filter all judgement and discernment and perception through your lens of self by necessity.

So many of the clients I speak with have been bewitched by this word *selfish* and its connotations—especially loving, caring, compassionate, empathetic women like this client. People have received the memo loud and clear that selfishness is one of the worst attributes. It denotes a myriad of unwelcome qualities—meanness, arrogance, insensitivity. Even worse, it is overlaid with virtue judgements. It's morally reprehensible to be self-ish. But you cannot actually be self-less!

If you were literally without a sense of self or ego, you would not have a way to focus your consciousness. There would be no banks through which the rivers of your consciousness could flow, as it were. On a metaphysical level, you might say that there could be no humanity through which your spirituality could flow. In the dreamscape, and only in the dreamscape, you *have* released your ego, but in waking hours we are all egocentric. So, when all was said and done, my client had ascribed to the social narrative about overt selfishness being morally bad. You are bad when you unapologetically pursue your own needs. You are bad when you state blatantly what you want. You are bad when you unashamedly put your-self first. This is why her sexual partner had unwittingly attracted the selfish label.

But my client had become caught in the proverbial briar patch, because she too was being selfish. She was also benefitting from the relationship. She was drawn to the passion and connection, she sincerely liked this person, and she was fulfilling her own selfish desires too. But she was reluctant to admit this to herself because it contradicted her idea of herself. She knew herself to be kind and helpful and giving and loving and compassionate—all the good things. But when she pursued her own sexual gratification and wanted connection for the mere pleasure of connection, these were thrown into the bad basket in her mind. These things were selfish.

It's bad to be like him, she'd think. *He's just out for himself. He's a bad guy. "* she'd think *"He's selfish and greedy, but I'm not. I'm good.* Under these circumstances, her natural and normal and psychologically healthy and spiritually savvy self-ishness needed to employ some guerrilla warfare. It needed to go underground. Hence it became stealth-selfishness.

Bear in mind that her self-hood did not go anywhere. She could mistake an asset for a liability, but Spirit doesn't. Spirit wants you to be in human form. Spirit wants you to be you while you're here. Spirit wants to flow your consciousness through you and your individual and unique and personal perspective. But in a culture that often denigrates people for overt selfhood, even going so far as to suggest there is psychopathy involved (i.e. narcissism), natural and necessary selfhood becomes tacit and furtive.

Some people have taken this social directive so much to heart that they chronically live in what is commonly known as selflessness. But remember, we have reworked this notion of self-less-ness such that it is rendered meaningless. Human beings cannot be without self, but they can erroneously believe they are. They can also come to believe this is honourable.

So to be more precise, some people are chronically living in stealth-selfishness. They are operating through the lens of self and holding personal desires and personal opinions and personal preferences but not openly admitting these to others or themselves. I know many who are gifted healers, who are masterful comforters, who are extraordinary carers. It's like they are the most magnificent firefighters—the most eager to rescue, the most eager to help. Indeed, there is a powerful, sincere desire within them to be helpful and giving. Day after day, month after month, year after year they arrive on the symbolic scene of the fire and foolishly push their way through, proclaiming, "Here I am ... let me in there ... I want to help!" They throw aside all care and concern for self amid protests and beseeching from colleagues to "just wait a moment ... put on your oxygen mask, wear your suit ... take care of yourself first."

These figurative rescuers—these caring, giving men and women—believe that it is selfish to stop and protect themselves under any conditions. If they are asked to overwork, they will do it. If they are asked to bake the class cupcakes, they will do it. If they are asked to chair a meeting, they will do it, whether they want to or not, whether it's convenient or not. These individuals emerge from every proverbial rescue more and more depleted. It's like the years of smoke inhalation have charred their lungs, the third-degree burns are becoming first-degree, and it is understood that, inevitably and before too long, they will be burnt to a cinder.

It is not noble to chronically people-please. The reason I argue for a notion of stealth-selfishness rather than genuine self-less-ness is because, without fail, every client who is tarred with the brush of the chronic helper *does* harbour personal preferences. These individual *do* want to say no when they say yes. They will often help under false pretences, well aware that they have given false impressions. While they may deny their own self, their own personal desire is bubbling furiously within them. Their own individual want will lay dormant for a while, but it does eventually erupt. It erupts in anger or resentment or bitterness or depression or heart disease or migraines or chronic fatigue or comfort eating or smoking.

The self that you are is the Self that came forth from the heavens. It's the God-force within you. How you treat your-self, how you think about your-self, and how you talk about your-self is a direct reflection of how well you recognise your-self as the magnificent, important child of God that you are. Ultimately I would prefer we ditched the term *selfish*, because it has been marinating in pungent social juices for too long and all the nutrients have leached out of it. The term *self-full* is better in my opinion, because there is no greater compliment you can pay than to proclaim to somebody, "You are so full of your-self"—that is, "You are so full of Spirit."

Now I think it may be fair to presume that some people will have a hard time interchanging selfish for Spirit-ish. I can hear you saying, "Well, that's all well and good, Deidre. Yeah, I intellectually get what you're saying. Sure, ego and self are synonymous, and *selfish* can simply mean your sense of your-self rather than mean or inconsiderate or rude. But aren't we just playing with semantics here? There are still mean behaviours. Inconsiderate behaviour is still a thing, no matter what you call it."

Firstly I would say touché, young Padawan. You are indeed paying attention, and secondly I would say that you are making a fair point. If we go back to our example, you could easily say that our young man was inconsiderate when he did not respect my client's request to stop text-messaging. While you are indeed demonstrating psychological aptitude to suspect that there is still such a thing as inconsiderate behaviour, you are not demonstrating psychological mastery with such an inquiry. Psychological mastery is akin to spiritual mastery, and spiritual mastery calls you to love unconditionally. What I explained to my client was that she was making an error on two levels. She was not only placing him into a wrong category, her judgement and blame of him were coming from an angry place within herself. As a result, her perceptions were doubly mistaken.

This is a common error made within intimate relationships as well as parental relationships. Parents, especially regarding teenage children, can categorise certain behaviour as wrong, and because teenagers will often refuse to mollify their parents by doing right (at least according to their parents' criteria), parents become angry in response. Anger, I'm sorry to say, makes you blind. There is a now a painful, perpetual loop established:

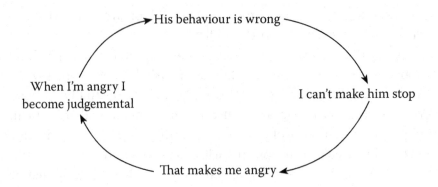

I pointed out to my client that whenever people make a judgement from a place of anger, they essentially have blinkers on. If you are in anger, you are out of love. As we explored in previous chapters, standing on the emotional step of anger is not bad in itself, and it can be the first step back to empowerment. But anger is not love. Anger, albeit normal and necessary sometimes, is not your highest nature. When your angry child screams "I hate you" you don't need to react as if your child is a font of wisdom and - in that very moment - they are uttering their most profound haiku. If an angry teenager yells "you don't love me anymore" you don't need to respond as if they are a fountain of clarity and - in that very moment - they are offering their most profound soliloquy. Anger is just a bit crazy! When anger is on the rampage parents or partners or co-workers can often stick around and debate with it rather than lovingly, confidently and compassionately disengaging and waiting until crazy has left the building! As my client came to discover you cannot perceive another human being accurately when you stand outside of love, compassion, grace, or mercy. Every war across history has demonstrated this fact.

This point became particularly evident to my client when I suggested that if she flipped the paradigm and imagined her partner telling himself a very similar story to the one she was presently telling me, he could equally accuse her of dishonesty and misrepresentation because she had gone back on her word too. In one breath, she had asked him not to contact her, and in the next she was replying to his text message. The basis of what I was saying was that, if he jumped up onto his soapbox and proclaimed her to be a liar and a game-player, these angry judgements or bitter accusations on his part would be littered with inaccuracies. While you can understand how he might end up with an impression that she was fickle or playing him, you can equally appreciate that he would be mistaken.

She could see this clearly when she got a degree of distance. She knew herself to be well meaning and well intentioned, yet she also appreciated that her behaviour might not portray this to onlookers. She understood that he could perceive her hesitancy as game-playing, and he could easily mistake her ambivalence for lying. He might even take her comfort-seeking for selfishness. As soon as you make it your assignment to psychoanalyze another person's motives and agenda, and you are doing it from a glass house of wrongness and a high horse of self-righteous anger, you are spiritually and psychologically blind. You have forgotten your own spiritual assignment, which is to love as purely, as deeply, and as frequently as possible.

My client had expressed some hesitance about this idea of unconditional love, as many do. Her ideas of love were exactly that: ideas. Moreover, they were Westernised, socially constructed ideas, and you know what I think about those. Her idea of love made her think that she would become a doormat—that loving him meant allowing him to dictate the terms of the relationship because that would please him. To her, loving him meant staying with him under the conditions *he* preferred. She had taken the mandate "don't be selfish" to mean "be selfless"— surrender your own preferences for another and slap a "love" sticker over it. Ironically, the reverse is true when you understand what love actually is. Loving unconditionally simply means not categorising another as wrong. She could step out of anger and notions of wrong and view him purely as a guy living his life on his own terms, in the best way he knew how.

Now be wary here. You don't need to overlay your idea of your best way with his best way. Don't be tempted to insert that old chestnut, "But I would never do that. I'd never be in multiple relationships at the same time." I'm sure you've personally sat with the discomfort of others trying to assert their own values onto you because they are adamant you are wrong. I'm sure you have personally experienced another person presuming to understand your motives and being vehement about your guilt. I'm sure you've personally encountered another person presuming to know the depth and complexity of who you are and then rejecting you. The Truth of who you are is inscrutable and loving, eternal and good-hearted, and simply a matter of doing your best as often as you can. Why then would you ever feel entitled to make negative judgements against another?

As I pointed out to my client, she could assert her preference for a monogamous, long-term relationship in an empowered manner without needing to make him wrong or bad in the process. Paradoxically, when she released notions of wrong, she was immediately less angry. As it turns out, it wasn't his behaviour that was making her angry, it was merely holding herself out of love and acceptance, out of mercy and compassion. When you stand in fear and judgement, for *any* reason, you are simply standing in fear and judgement. This runs so counter to your spiritual nature, as well as your natural psychology, that you instinctively want to shift out of it.

If my client had held herself in anger until this scoundrel changed his behaviour, she could have been waiting indefinitely. Empowering herself to own her preferences without guilt or anger ironically allowed her to discontinue the relationship much more easily. She became the change agent by stepping off the merry-go-round of pain. She focused upon the thing that she could change: herself. This transformation could only take place when she reoriented her focus towards self. When she realised that all events in her life literally orbited about her and she alone was the focal point for all events within her own life, she could see that it was up to her to decide how she was going to use this gravitational pull.

You are literally the centre of your own universe. You are the sole heir within your own mind. It's just you and You in there, 24/7. You have a choice as to the type of universe you create, and you can only create for yourself. You can decide to be like a sun with a gravitational pull that draws heavenly people and delightful experiences to you as you radiate light and warmth out into your universe, or you can decide to be more like a black hole. Same gravitational pull, but instead of sending *out* light and warmth and love, you draw *in* all the light and warmth that happens to trip into your vicinity. My client decided she would much prefer being a sun to being a black hole. When she owned her preferences without guilt or anger or fear, she instinctively and easily knew what she wanted.

Kids know that they are the centre of their own universe, and they also understand that it could be no other way. I have spent a great deal of this section exploring and extrapolating the perils and pitfalls of selflessness and deconstructing the idea of *selfish* from an adult's perspective, because it's adults who become entangled in concepts of selfishness and ego, and as a result find themselves stuck in guilt and resentment. Kids just aren't entwined in it like we are. While they are young enough to avoid the muddle, they do not experience guilt about their personal desires. They understand that their personal wants do not impinge upon another person's, and they are comfortable enough to assert their preferences.

Now I could be presumptuous and guess that you may disagree with the sentiment that one's personal wants do not impinge upon another person's. But you must understand that your empowerment is always aligned with the empowerment of those around you. It's like Spirit is constantly sprinkling the perfect combination of salt and pepper into every situation. However, people become confused about the idea that one person's happiness can interfere with or limit or restrict another person's happiness because *happy* has become one of those misunderstood words. I know, it's a linguistic minefield out there. It does seem to most people like their happiness can be at the expense of another, and this was the false premise upon which my client was making her argument: "He is making himself happy, and that's making me unhappy."

Let's take a scenario in which parents might believe their child's preferences impinge upon a sibling's. What if my six-year-old son wanted to go to the park and my eight-year-old wanted to stay home playing on his iPad? You could be forgiven for thinking these are competing desires, because on the surface it would appear they are in opposition. Perhaps a more relatable example would be if you and a partner were holding apparently contradictory desires. Let's inject some controversy and say perhaps you wanted to have children but your partner did not. What if we took away the notion of *happy*—"Having a child will make me happy, I can't have a child because of my partner, therefore I can't be happy"—and substituted the word *empower*—"Having a child will empower me." *Empower me* can mean "bring me fun," "bring me a challenge," "bring me growth," "bring me insight," "bring me excitement," "bring me contentment."

As our hopeful mother-to-be gains confidence and starts to become assertive about her unwavering desire, our hesitant father-don't-wanna-be is given an opportunity to practice compassion and humility. It's not that one person's desire trumps another's, simply that both parties are called to practice empowerment in its various forms. As one party gains in authenticity and becomes more self-full, the other party is given a psychological assignment to become more flexible and accepting. As one party gains tentative courage, maybe even demonstrating anger or making errors of judgement, the other party is given the opportunity to practice grace and mercy. Confidence, assertiveness, acceptance, humility, authenticity, self-full-ness, flexibility, compassion, courage, anger, poor judgement, grace, mercy ... there is no end to the facets of this extraordinary human experience. All of it is good and necessary and worthwhile and empowering.

Our scenario is not all happy-making, certainly, and by framing it as such we'd easily become entangled in notions of happiness scarcity. If you get to be happy, I won't get to be happy. One person needs to sacrifice happiness for the other. But when we frame the predicament as empowering for both parties, then it is *all* empowering. Having a complimentary nature to another person is not a problem to be tackled but a gift to be embraced—salt and pepper, not oil and water, not chalk and cheese.

A woman who desperately wants a baby with a partner who does not is faced with any number of spiritual and psychological opportunities, none of which are wrong or bad, just empowering. She could choose to honour her own desire and leave. Painful? Probably. Empowering? Absolutely. She could hold herself apart from her desire, believing it to be nice while simultaneously feeling angry and bitter. Painful? Yes. An opportunity for empowerment and enlightenment? Of course. She could surrender the problem to the Universe and prayerfully trust that all will be revealed. Painful? Perhaps. Enlightened? Yes. She could peacefully release her own desire, deciding that she can live a thrilling and fulfilling life with her partner. Painful? Maybe. Empowering? Yes. There is no script here. There is no right, and there can be no wrong. It simply boils down to one individual making a powerful choice for his or her own unique life experience.

Likewise, empowered parenting is not about an undiscerning yes or a mechanical no. Kids are robust and resilient enough to hear a disappointing no as well as optimistic and confident enough to expect an enthusiastic yes. Kids are wise enough to understand that they hold the right to express their unique, personal perspective regardless of how others might respond. When my six-year old wants to go to the park and we do, my eight-year-old is presented with an opportunity to collaborate and be flexible, while my six-year-old is given an opportunity to be gracious when things go his way. My eight-year-old could take this empowerment opportunity and find happiness in someone else's preference—or not. He could just as easily choose to be sullen and grumpy. My eight-year-old could decide that my six-year-old is selfish and favoured and life is unfair, while my six-year-old may gloat and crow and believe himself deserving. Or vice versa. There are any number of variations and combinations all ready to be mined for the gold that is there.

Every eventuality is guaranteed to be empowering. Empowering in ways that feel good? Not likely. Empowering in ways that don't feel so good? Probably. Even situations that appear on the surface to be disempowering are really just empowerment in disguise. Feelings of disempowerment simply offer opportunities to make your way back to empowerment. Whether you're at basecamp or on the summit of Everest, you are always on the mountain. Whether you have found bliss and peace on your path or your path has led you into a deep, depressing, foreboding forest, you are still on your path.

To be blunt and plain, in Truth there are really just variations of good and right, from a spiritual and psychological perspective. Are you loving in this moment? Yes? That's great and probably hugely satisfying and a lot of fun. Are you loving in this moment? No? That's fine too; you're probably not having as much fun but here's a golden opportunity to come back to your loving nature, and that *can* be fun! It's all good. It's all right. When you understand that you are indeed the centre of your own universe, you pay closer attention to the galaxy that you personally want to create for yourself.

Ultimately, empowered parenting is about balance. It's about yin and yang. It's about meta parenting and recognising how restrictive and inhibiting social ideologies do not serve personal empowerment. It's about honouring children as unique individuals, not lumps of clay to thwack into socially acceptable moulds. It's about respecting the pure, unfettered God-force that children are.

I like to imagine the self as being like a long, gorgeous, couture coat. To be clear, I'm describing the self here—your sense of self, your self-image—not your God-Self, not your Spirit. When you enter into a life, this coat that you wear is unblemished. It's clean and clear, it's ever so comfortable, and it fits perfectly. As you begin to move through life, the coat starts to get a little dirty. Some of the muck is simply picked up from stumbling and bumbling through muddy puddles along your own personal path. The hem gets a bit tatty and grubby, but all is well because this is just a part of the journey.

As your path takes you through villages and towns, the coat gets really filthy, but it's not the inevitable, occasional puddles—it's naysayers and critics and hecklers standing on the sidelines hurtling handfuls of mud: "be thinner," "be smarter," "be nicer," "be sensible," "be original," "be like us," "be on our side," "be strong," "be quiet." Before too long, the coat has become encrusted with mud. Over time it congeals, making the coat stiff and scratchy, uncomfortable and restrictive. Occasionally you happen upon a pond or river, and you make an attempt to clean the coat, bringing it back to its former glory, but you just can't seem to get more than ten paces without somebody slinging another handful of mud. The hecklers are waiting at work, the critics are lurking on the TV, the naysayers are amassing at the family barbecue. Your sense of self can feel so clogged and hardened that you become uncomfortable in it. Some people will discard it altogether, and we call that suicide.

A tight, shrunken, inflexible self depresses you. It makes you angry, and you feel hopeless and powerless. You are in desperate need of a dry-cleaner, but the holy water isn't necessarily in the cathedral or the temple like you were told. My point is, rather than accepting that life is inescapably cruddy, we could decide to just stop slinging so much shit on each other. A self that is in a shambles and is repugnant is what you might call criminal or defiant or narcissistic or antisocial or selfish or rude... or.... or.... or.... I would say it's just a grubby self-image, a mucky ego, and we just need to get thee to a dry-cleaner.

Challenge yourself to pay closer attention to those who walk among us whose self is cleaner and less blemished. They stand three feet tall with dirt under their fingernails, jam around their mouths, and mismatched shoes. They may not even know how to use the toilet properly, but they've sure rockin' something pretty damn special. Their brilliance lies in the fact that they don't yet think like an adult. While it's a sad indictment of Western culture, that fact makes them more spiritually savvy and psychologically masterful that the average grown-up.

CHAPTER 11

Revising Psychological Diagnoses: Let's Start With ADHD and ODD

The Diagnostic and Statistical Manual of Mental Disorders (DSM-5) is published by the American Psychiatric Association and is in its fifth revision. It purports to offer psychologists, doctors, and psychiatrists standard criteria for the classification of mental disorders. Psychologists are trained very thoroughly in its use as well as in the use of many other diagnostic instruments.

As you have probably already gathered, I take issue with the bulk of traditional psychology because it views the human experience as the convergence of thoughts, feelings, and behaviours. In my opinion, this excludes the most dominant component, which is the spiritual nature. But just as importantly, like medicine, it takes this human gestalt and filters it through a construct of pathology or disease. The psychological house of cards is built upon a foundation of brokenness and original sin.

Now don't misunderstand: I'm not saying that people don't experience psychological challenges. Yes, depression happens; yes, anxiety happens; yes, people feel hopeless and suicidal and stressed and enraged. Yes, yes, I know. But many individuals have been led to build their houses on sand because they deeply believe that the foundation of their personhood is cracked and in need of inevitable reinforcement. People's sense of self is fragile. They feel like unworthiness lurks about every corner, ready to pounce upon them at the next sign of disapproval from a partner or co-worker. They worry that at their core, at the deepest place within their psyche, lurks unworthiness. They believe themselves to be fundamentally flawed, or stupid, or pointless, or ugly.

Within the symbolic house that is a person's psychology, experiences of depression or anxiety or anger could be naturally overcome intuitively and confidently. It's as straightforward as demolishing one wall and relocating it. Experiences of trauma and abuse could even be naturally overcome intuitively and confidently. It may not be as simple a job. Perhaps it involves the demolition of a whole room or even gutting the place and revamping the entire interior—hard work, it's true, but still achievable. But when you come upon a house where the foundation is crumbling, it does you no good to replace the walls or demolish a room. You need to address the foundational problem.

Society begot medicine and medicine begot psychology, and this lineage carries a common rogue gene: worthlessness. The human creature has been traditionally regarded as evil or sinful or sick or insane or worthless for millennia. So when people come to me struggling with depression or anxiety or trauma or anger, I need to climb under the house and check the condition of the foundation. Do they believe themselves to be fundamentally priceless? Do they believe themselves to be worthless at their foundation? Do they know their spiritual nature? Often people aren't just making cosmetic alterations to their metaphorical house structure—knocking out this wall here and exposing the brickwork there—but they also believe that the footings are cracked and broken.

Where would they have picked up this nonsensical idea? Culturally we believe that a person *can* lose his or her innate value. Such narratives abound throughout our history and continue today. The sheer idea that a human being can be crazy or monstrous or evil or bad flies in the face of every spiritual Truth known, yet it's perpetuated ad nauseam. This is the fatal flaw in traditional psychology—this tacit presumption that human beings not just *can* be broken but often *are*. The inception of psychology as a discipline followed on the heels of the medical model, so medical pathology simply morphed into psychopathology; medical dis-ease mutated into mental dis-order.

Let me give you a couple of broad examples about the profundities of you as a magnificent human to see if I can emphasise why any idea to the contrary is so ridiculous. Have you ever thought about what your mind is? It is your experience of your consciousness—literally your sense of your self, this thing that is so deeply and inextricably tied to your human experience that you might not have given it a second thought. But here is an interesting thing to think about: You know your brain to be physical in nature, a complex, magnificent clump of neurons, dendrites ... you know ... fancy brain stuff. But what is your mind in relationship to that clump of biology?

Doctors and surgeons and pathologists and coroners will perform surgery and autopsy and diagnostics in order to elucidate this mind–brain connection. It is really hard to fathom how something as undefinable as your mind somehow emanates from the mushy, jelly-like substance that is your brain. Modern medicine and modern science have not found any satisfying way to describe how, when you close your eyes, you can literally transport yourself anywhere. You can literally imagine anything using your mind's eye. Your mind has its own eye—what is up with that?

Brain and mind are somehow so indivisibly linked yet are seemingly so separate. Acquired brain injuries sustained in specific regions of the brain have concrete effects on specific skill like speech and sight or movement. Meanwhile, there seems to be no as-yet tangible connection between the brain and dreams or the brain and intuition or the brain and psychic abilities. We can simply make imprecise and rudimentary efforts to understand this inscrutable connection, such as the study of the sleep state, from rapid eye movement to alpha and delta waves. But can we possibly conceive of the dreamscape in purely physical terms? The various phenomena of consciousness—dreams, the mind's eye, hypnotic states, trance, imagination—these characteristics of humanity are simply not well understood by science or medicine.

Here is another amazing thing that your psychology can accomplish, which is taken for granted by medicine and science, yet cannot be explained by either (because you are just that cool): the placebo effect. When you really think about it, the placebo effect is one of the most exquisite proofs of you psychological prowess, and yet it's often relegated to the "oh yeah ... that thing ... so what" corner. It is taken for granted in scientific and medical circles as an "effect." Yet if you could allow yourself to revel in this miraculous occurrence, you might not be so complacent about it.

Science and medicine will often relegate such "miracles" to the back corner. But think about this. It is clearly known and well established that the power of your expectation can be so strong it is enough to influence your physiology. Keep in mind, this is not the power of denial; in a controlled trial where a placebo is administered, participants aren't told "This won't work, but just pretend as hard as you can that it will." It is not the power of fantasy; participants aren't told "This placebo won't help you but just act like it has—act your way into wellness." No. Placebo is the power of your mind to *expect* wellness. It is the power of your mind to *expect* benefit. It is literal evidence of how powerful you are when you have conviction and positive expectations. Within a spiritual framework, such phenomena are not considered miraculous at all. It is just given that the power of Source can heal an incurable illness as easily as a dog scratching off a flea.

Outside of a spiritual framework, such phenomena does seem extraordinary. Scientists and doctors grope about, either indifferent to these unexplainables or trying to work them into the medical paradigm. Leaving Spirit out of the human gestalt is tantamount to leaving petrol out of a car. The mechanic might know how to service the car, and he might look under the hood and tell you how it runs, and he can even restore its functioning, but without appreciating the importance of the petrol, you've not got much.

Medicine and science began with the study of the human body's physicality, and from this marriage psychiatry and psychology were born—the study of the human mind. Dr. Rupert Sheldrake speaks eloquently from a meta perspective about the sciences in his TED talk "The Science Delusion," and he echoes the sentiment that science is built upon a foundation of materialism. He goes on to reaffirm that the default belief system of most educated adults is that the universe is mechanistic, matter is unconscious, the universe is fixed and purposeless, and psychic phenomena are illusions.

Obviously, I would strongly agree with and extend Dr. Sheldrake's viewpoint to say that it is not only science and medicine but also psychology that carries within its shared heritage the advancements and limitations of this medico-scientific parentage. Medicine and science seemed to made good bedfellows, while religion (or at least spirituality) became the clandestine mistress. Medicine and spirituality may have birthed a bastard child here and there, and science and spirituality might have even had some furtive meetings of their own, but they were largely kept separate. Psychology has not felt adventurous enough to seriously inquire into psychic and spiritual realms, so sweeping portions of the human experience have either been ignored entirely, disparaged and minimised, or reworked to fit into the narrow arena of the physical.

I would suggest to you that, through the lens of spiritual psychology, there are several diagnoses that would be radically reconfigured and re-envisioned. Bipolar disorder, schizophrenia and psychoses, addictions, suicidality, dissociative disorders, antisocial personality and social anxieties, and of course ADHD (attention deficit hyperactivity disorder) and ODD (oppositional defiant disorder) would be turned on their heads. The DSM-5 diagnostic criteria for ADHD are as follows:

People with ADHD show "a persistent pattern of inattention and/or hyperactivity-impulsivity that interferes with functioning or development as characterised by (1) and/or (2):

1. **Inattention: Six or more symptoms have persisted for at least 6 months to a degree that is inconsistent with developmental level and that negatively impacts directly on social and academic/occupational activities:**

- Often fails to give close attention to details or makes careless mistakes in schoolwork, at work, or during other activities.
- Often has difficulty sustaining attention on tasks or play activities.
- Often does not seem to listen when spoken to directly.
- Often does not follow through on instructions and fails to finish schoolwork, chores, or duties in the workplace (e.g., loses focus, side-tracked).
- Often has difficulty organising tasks and activities.
- Often avoids, dislikes, or is reluctant to engage in tasks that require mental effort (such as schoolwork or homework).
- Often loses things necessary for tasks and activities (e.g. school materials, pencils, books, tools, wallets, keys, paperwork, eyeglasses, mobile telephones).
- Is often easily distracted by extraneous stimuli.
- Is often forgetful in daily activities.

2. **Hyperactivity and Impulsivity: Six or more of the following symptoms have persisted for at least 6 months to a degree that is inconsistent with developmental level and that negatively impacts directly on social and academic/ occupational activities:**

- Often fidgets with or taps hands or feet, or squirms in seat.
- Often leaves seat in situations when remaining seated is expected.
- Often runs about or climbs in situations where it is inappropriate (adolescents or adults may be limited to feeling restless).
- Often unable to play or take part in leisure activities quietly.
- Is often "on the go" acting as if "driven by a motor."
- Often talks excessively.
- Often blurts out an answer before a question has been completed.

- Often has trouble waiting his/her turn.
- Often interrupts or intrudes on others (e.g., butts into conversations or games)."

Cast your mind back to previous chapters and think about the examples I offered of how differently children and adults think. Take two of the examples I gave: the fact that children will orient themselves towards fun and ease much more easily than adults and that children are naturally inclined to live in the Now. As adults, we recognise how advantageous it is to be happy, and in ever-increasing numbers we are recognising the astonishing power of Now. But when children offer a living picture of how this spiritual and psychological mastery is accomplished from moment to moment, we seem befuddled by it.

I used to be a strict parent. I was raised by strict parents, and I adopted many of their parenting ideologies. Recently I saw a parent responding to a child in much the same way as I used to. A father was dropping his sons off at school. His boys must have been about eight and thirteen, at a guess. The exchange I noticed was very brief, but it reminded me so much of my past parenting style. Initially, I heard this father in the parking lot. His son had walked beside their car, and the dad boomed, "Get off the road!" My reaction was one of shock—not for what was said, but the volume of it. It was definitely attention-grabbing. I too used to speak in a commanding tone like that, using that kind of volume. I would say that I "barked" at my kids often, and I took it as firm, authoritative parenting.

The three of them proceeded to walk to the classroom. Along the way, they needed to negotiate a crosswalk. Again the child found himself scolded because as he walked slightly ahead of his dad, he was about to cross just as a car was rolling up to the crosswalk. There was a teacher on duty standing at the ready with a stop sign, and the driver of the car had clearly seen the gaggle of people approaching the crossing and the car was cruising to a gentle hault. However, I again heard the father, in a much lower voice but with that gruff, guttural disapproval, say, "Wait!"

Strike three came as they walked across the lawn. Our father had veered off the footpath and was walking a slightly tangential route.

He began calling the boy by name: "Jacob." His voice was relatively quiet now but it carried the same insistent, growling tone. The young man was having none of it, and he was sticking to his chosen route along the footpath. The father was now maintaining a more restrained volume because more people were milling about, but his voice lost none of its authority: "Jacob." Again his son ignored him, refusing to yield. The other child knew enough to keep his head down and avoid eye contact. He scuttled to his classroom, happy to be outside of the fallout zone. The final order was given: "Jacob!" By now, Jacob was almost out of earshot—or at least he was pretending that he was. He could continue with his bluff, making his way to class, leaving his dad at risk of social faux pas by publically humiliating an eight-year-old— or he could concede and make his way over to his dad, saving face and probably saving himself a belated punishment later on. He graciously chose the latter. His body language spoke volumes as he lumbered over to his father with his head hung and shoulders stooped. "Where is your head at?" his dad criticised. *An interesting question*, I thought to myself, and I went about my business.

Now, this entire exchange took only a matter of minutes—five at maximum. I was privy to it only because my own route happened to run parallel. But it gave me food for thought that day because I have stood in the shoes of that father. I have asserted control and dominance over my children in the name of good parenting. And while my kids learned to obey me, I suspect they learned little else. There was a time when I would have consoled myself with the notion that they learned to respect authority or to exert self-control or self-discipline or to feel self-respect or even to display good manners. Nowadays, I'm just not sure that's true. I have seen that look of intimidation on the faces of my children—and we aren't even talking about aggressive behaviour here, just scenarios like the one I've described.

I'm sure you have witnessed—or, like me, have been the conspirator of—just such a situation. It is seemingly so innocuous, and some perceive it as beneficial. But in recent times, I'm more inclined to demand less from my children and allow more. I have probably made a 180-degree turn and gone from strict to lax in the opinion of bystanders. I'm more likely to think about things from the child's perspective now, and it's an interesting two-way mirror when you can appreciate the parent's dilemma and simultaneously understand the child's predicament.

The young man in my story could easily be regarded as defiant—but only from an adult perspective. Defiance implies malice, defiance implies manipulation, defiance implies spite. Indeed, I have spoken with clients who ascribe malice and manipulation to a child as young as three. But a three-year-old is *not* malicious and spiteful. Parents can be oppositional, so they presume their children can be too. Parents have forgotten what it is like within the psychology of a five- or nine- or thirteen-year-old. They become prisoners within their own adult mind because their perceptions are trapped within this adult perspective.

From this young man's perspective, I can imagine his confusion as to why such a big fuss was made over such small things. He was easy-going and self-full, not irresponsible. I can imagine this boy wondering how he could possibly please his father and not necessarily grasping what he had even done wrong. He was confused and annoyed, not malicious. I can also imagine this boy working psychologically to "turn the other cheek"—that is to say, I can imagine him effectively ignoring his father, selectively hearing whatever he was psychologically able to tolerate at the time. He was making efforts to remain buoyed and was becoming defensive, but at no point was he bad.

Imagine a scenario in which our father reproached, "Where's your head at?" and our young man retorted, "You're right, Dad, I'm being an idiot." Even posing the question is a lose-lose situation for our father and son. When you distil the essence of this question, it is simply asking, "Why are you being 'bad'?" How can there possibly be a psychologically satisfying answer to that loaded question? Behind Door #1, the son might answer, "Yes, Dad, I'm sorry, I should listen." While our father believes this to be the answer he's seeking, the energy of this answer is disempowered, the spirit of it is powerlessness, and it smacks of guilt. I predict that while it may satisfy our father's self-righteous intellect, it pangs the heart.

Behind Door #2, the son might become angry and begin to argue his case: "I was listening." I expect that he would be very quickly interrupted with, "No, you weren't, you stepped on the road and then walked in front of that car, and then you didn't come when I asked." Perhaps the boy would succumb to the pressure, offer a perfunctory "Sorry, Dad," and be on his way, still seething in anger. Or maybe he would offer a rebuttal: "I was just getting my bag ... I didn't see a car ... I'm just walking to class." "No, no, no." "Yes, yes, yes." (sounds like as much fun as dental surgery with a rusty fork doesn't it?). Either way, we are psychologically reaping either embarrassment and guilt or anger and resentment.

Behind Door #3, the son might become apathetic and indifferent. He might not say anything and be wise enough to keep his opinions to himself. This is the lesser of the three evils, and indeed it was the path the boy took. Rather than choosing Door #1, where the prize was powerlessness, or Door #2, where the prize was anger or guilt, he opted for Door #3, where the prize was indifference. As far as it goes, he intuitively found his way to the least crappy option. It is relatively easy to spiritually and psychologically move from indifference and apathy to hope and happiness.

I could imagine this young man going to class, still feeling annoyed, and venting to his mates. His loyal friends would rally around him, employing the psychological tools of sarcasm and bravado and distraction. Then the matter would be put to rest. Sure, defiance might be a nuisance, but isn't it preferable to worthlessness? Yeah, indifference may be disconcerting, but isn't it preferable to anger and guilt? I guess the answer to those questions will depend upon whether you would rather be right or happy.

With an understanding of what spiritual and psychological mastery is, and the fact that children have a bead on it, I am deeply troubled by diagnostics, especially applied to children, that pathologise any manifestation of their experience. Wording like "often fails to give close attention to ..." "often has trouble holding attention on ..." "often does not seem to listen when ..." "often does not follow through on ..." troubles me. My allegiance tends to lie with children first and foremost, because I understand that as screwy as things might have become for them, they've been here for a shorter period of time, and their manifestation of *screwy* probably isn't as screwy as our adult versions of screwy.

I hold deep misgivings when adults proclaim that their children won't listen to them. My instinct calls me to ask, "What are you expecting them to listen to, exactly?" I harbour deep reservations when adults proclaim that their children won't do as they are told. My intuition makes me wonder, "What are you telling them to do, exactly?" There is a hidden agenda within these diagnostics, and in my opinion this renders them highly suspect.

For the sake of clarification, I'm not suggesting that inattention within children isn't an issue and that it can't impact on functioning. I'm a clinical psychologist, and I often witness first-hand how functioning is impacted on a day-to-day basis by all manner of psychological milieux. Nevertheless, I am suspicious of a system that declares a child to be a problem. I appreciate that parents become understandably frustrated, justifiably frazzled, and reasonably confused, but within our society, the notion of a "problem child" is bolstered even to the point of medication. Parents, educators, doctors, and even psychologists are toiling under the same social norms, because we ourselves are a product of these social norms. Unless and until you are enlightened and empowered enough to look critically at these social constructs—strengthened with grandiose terminology and elevated to the elite professional to diagnose—then we are often just perpetuating archaic dogma rather than evolving into genuine new frontiers.

As radical as it may sound, I am inclined to ask if a child is fundamentally happy. Generally, before we proceed, I need to deconstruct with clients what I mean by "happy." Remember, we are talking empowered happy, viscerally happy, fiercely happy. Is your child aligned with his or her Source, love, Self? No? Then let's rectify that as our priority and then talk about inattention issues (if they are still a problem at that stage). Is your child happy? Maybe. Then let's ensure that firstly and talk about the other secondly (if it's still a problem). Is your child predominantly happy? Yes. Then let's talk about the inattention within the broader context of happiness and empowerment. When this foundation is solid, you can rip up the whole house and start again if you want to and it's not a major problem. All things are possible when this foundation is solid.

It is my assertion that inattention is easily misinterpreted by adults—particularly frazzled or overwhelmed adults, or dare I say prideful or self-righteous adults—and it's easily misconstrued as rudeness or misbehaviour. Many adults do not understand for themselves the psychological benefits of turning the other cheek. Said differently, adults do not often understand the benefits of selective hearing or downright ignoring. The majority of clients I see who are struggling with anxiety do not know how to do healthy psychological inattention—self-protective ignoring. I have spoken with many, many clients who are overly concerned with the opinion of others, who will give their attention to other people's evaluations and choose their actions and reactions on this basis. This awareness—the awareness of what other people want and think—does not serve them.

I was speaking to a client recently who was in the midst of a divorce. His wife was having an affair and eventually decided to end the marriage. This all came out of the blue for my client, and he was struggling to make a myriad of psychological adjustments. It was like he'd crossed from one familiar, comfortable world into a foreign, unknown world, and he was left reeling from the upheaval. One of the most troubling aspects for him was his ex-wife's behaviour. From his perception, she was casting him as the villain of the piece. Despite their divorce being solely at her behest, she was ostensibly being divisive among their mutual friends and sporting teams, bandying around salacious stories.

My client just couldn't find resonance with this mentality. His perspective of "I was unexpectedly left for another man with no recourse, and I thought I was a pretty good husband" was completely opposite to her perspective of "I left an unhappy marriage, perhaps in an undignified way, but he was a terrible husband and now I'm moving on." In order to justify or explain their anger or guilt, some people will cast you as the villain in their reality. They will not understand another's motives, words, sentiments, beliefs, or actions, and as a consequence, they may presume that others' motives are negative, and their words or opinions are wrong. But when one person casts another as a character in his or her own reality, there is no connection between the actual person and the avatar that has been formulated.

As humans, we are inclined towards simplified caricature rather than nuanced character. Hence our panache for categories like good or bad, right or wrong, villain or hero. My client was deeply unsettled with his casting in the villain role. He deeply and sincerely wanted to play the hero for others, and especially for his wife within his marriage. It was his awareness that others were now seeing him in this unflattering light that made him depressed and stressed and angry. He desperately wanted to plead his case, correct the flagrant inaccuracies, and set things right. Yet he knew the futility of trying to influence a crowd that was already boiling the tar and plucking the feathers.

Kids are able to stand more aloof from the misconceptions of others. This is, in part, due to their ability to not listen. Some kids are better at this than others; often, teenagers will utilise this tool to its full advantage, but the majority of kids will demonstrate this psychological mastery at one time or another. It is the classic example of an adult trying to discuss a child's mistakes or wrongdoings by emphatically ranting, "Look at what you did! ... Now why did you do that? ... Come over here! ... Listen when I'm speaking to you ... Take a look! ... Here. ... Here I said! ... Listen please. ... Will you come here and look? ... Why did you do this?" Children will psychologically duck and weave when you are trying to force their attention upon unwanted things. They will divert their eyes or split their attention or be generally inattentive; they may even seem to have a selective memory or selective hearing. This is not unhealthy avoidance. This is not unhealthy denial, it is positive denial.

I have experienced a divorce myself. I know first-hand what it's like to be misunderstood and how to successfully utilise the psychological tool that is positive denial. I initiated the divorce, and my ex-husband, much like my client, was understandably shocked and grief-stricken. Throughout the process, I was cast as the villain of the story. I know this was not done out of malice but simply out of ignorance. My ex-husband was not in a position to understand my motives, which were empowered and authentic for me but appeared selfish and callous to him. For a long time, he simply saw my behaviour as wrong, and I instinctively understood that I needed to disengage from his assessment of things. In order to remain psychologically buoyant, protect my empowerment, and most importantly hold to the most loving version of myself, I needed to detach. This was understandably viewed as coldness. It was seen as uncaring, and it was labelled ignoring.

Without this psychological defence mechanism, however, I might have sacrificed my empowerment. Buying into the rhetoric of wrong and bad is guilt-making and insecurity-making, and it saps you of your empowerment. Many of my clients, like society at large, do not grasp the profundity of turning the other cheek, and people are quick to label it negatively.

Now that I have given you food for thought regarding inattention, let us chew on the delectable concept of hyperactivity. As we have previously learned, one of the tricks the adult mind will play is telling you that because you are an intelligent being, you are logical, you are sensible, you are reasonable, and you will never think anything to yourself that is clearly irrational or obviously illogical. When people say to me, "Well, my mother is rude and critical," I reply, "That may be true." When people say to me, "Somebody might break into my house," "My business may go bankrupt," or "People might judge me," I retort "That may be true." When people say to me, "They did bully me at school," I say, "That may be true." The diabolical trick that the adult mind can play is convincing you that, because you are intelligent, you will not think anything that has *no* basis in truth. You've seen what you've seen, you've heard what you've heard, you've lived what you've lived.

But while your mind just wants to catalogue what's true, even if it means dwelling in anxiety or drowning in depression, your Spirit seeks a higher criteria. Your Spirit wants to focus upon what feels good. Happy is the order of the day. Love is the gold standard. The reason we can get so bogged down in depression or anxiety is that the adult mind is so convincing, it's so persuasive, it seems so accurate. And I say, "Of course you won't think anything to yourself that is obviously crazy," but where has all this intelligent observation gotten us? To depression, maybe; to anxiety, perhaps; to judgement and condemnation, certainly; to anger, absolutely; to misery, sometimes. It is like there's a constant duality: the truth as your mind and senses perceive it and the Truth as your Spirit feels it. It is the yin and the yang again.

Adults are frequently confronted by this dilemma: "Will I reside in the logical truth of what I saw, what I heard, what I lived, or will I teach myself to become illogically hopeful, irrationally loving, crazy optimistic, insanely joyful? Kids, especially more wild kids, can naturally reside in euphoric, blissful states. I can't help but be suspicious that such intense jubilation is easily mistaken for hyperactivity by tedious and stuffy adults who have forgotten that life is suppose to be magical and rapturous. Impulsivity could easily be reframed as invincibility, and when you are full of Spirit—as wild children often are—don't you want the rush of invulnerability, the thrill of freedom?

It's like these kids have tapped into natural opioids. They can fly so high that they become like ducks in mid-flight, shot down by the musket branded "cautious and sensible." Yes, in all things there must be balance. Let us say that's a given. But the idea of social standards masquerading as psychological disorder unsettles me. At the intersection of present-moment living, invincibility, positive denial, and easy/fun, we find the crux of ADHD. From a traditional psychological and medical standpoint, there is little benefit and little wisdom to be found in ADHD. From within a new paradigm—from a new psychological model that is tightly coupled to spiritual Truth— there is much gold to be mined from kids blessed with ADHD.

Now let's take a look at the diagnostic criteria for ODD. DSM-5 criteria for a diagnosis of ODD shows a:

pattern of angry/irritable mood, argumentative/defiant behaviour, or vindictiveness lasting at least 6 months as evidenced by at least four symptoms from any of the following categories, and exhibited during interaction with at least one individual who is not a sibling.

Angry and irritable mood:

- Often loses temper.
- Is often touchy or easily annoyed.
- Is often angry and resentful.

Argumentative/defiant behaviour:

- Often argues with authority figures or, for children and adolescents, with adults.
- Often actively defies or refuses to comply with requests from authority figures or with rules.
- Often deliberately annoys others.
- Often blames others for his or her mistakes or misbehaviour.

Vindictiveness:

- Has been spiteful or vindictive at least twice within the past six months. The disturbance in behaviour is associated with distress in the individual or others in his or her immediate social context (e.g., family, peer group, work colleagues) or it impacts negatively on social, educational, occupational or other important areas of functioning.

It is my hope that you are beginning to sense how and why I believe diagnoses like ADHD or conduct disorder or ODD are fatally flawed.

I hope you are beginning to appreciate how traditional psychology could overcome many of its limitations and forge into exciting and revolutionary new areas with an eye towards the spiritual. I will not spend too much time dissecting ODD here, as it is my intention to equip you with the tools for meta parenting such that you could cast your discerning eye over ODD and offer your own critique. I will just take a broad overview of the categories and offer some general, final thoughts.

I hope I have made it clear in previous chapters and sections that vindictiveness and defiance are in the eye of the beholder. Period. Let me now take on angry and irritable. Anger is a creative force. It is akin to the creative force of a tornado or a bush fire. There is a basic misunderstanding within Western culture about anger, because the destructive qualities are amplified and shunned, thereby muting the constructive potential. Many people I know would have a visceral reaction against the idea of a beautiful tornado or a creative bush fire—"Oh Deidre, you can't love a bush fire, what about the loss of life or the loss of homes or the loss of animals or land?" A similar premise is often used when individuals cite domestic violence as a rebuttal against embracing anger. In the same way, parents will often scold a child for *any* expression of anger. They will attempt to enforce a blanket ban, fearing that angry outbursts will inevitably lead to violence. *It just gets worse*, they fear.

I find that this general intimidation and fear about anger paradoxically incites anger. To assume that the most extreme instance of any given phenomena is contained within the most banal instance is an erroneous premise that is overused within our culture. It is fear-mongering on a massive scale, and our society attempts to eliminate unwanted experiences with these extremist arguments. Diets entail strict gastronomic regimes—eat *no* "bad" foods is the catch cry. Unsafe sex is ostensibly avoided with rhetoric about unwanted pregnancy, rape, and STD; have *no* sex is the tagline. Drugs and alcohol are quashed with narratives about imprisonment and death; take *no* drugs is the party line. While logical, these approaches are entirely invalid psychologically because they are lacking in balance. They run counter to our natural, splendid, wise psychology to such an extent that people are left attempting to do what is opposite to their nature. Assuming power and dominance over another person and delivering decrees does not psychologically empower; it does not psychologically motivate, and it provokes rebellion.

Trying to extinguish anger elicits an inevitable backlash, and anybody with psychological nous already knows this. Have we resolved obesity issues with a restrictive approach? Have we resolved sexual naivety with a punitive approach? Have we resolved drug or alcohol issues with an authoritarian approach? No. Not only that, the natural psychological benefits to anger, sexual exploration, drug curiosity, or pleasure-seeking are denied outright. This approach itself backfires and creates the problem of a drug culture, sexual disempowerment, or anger.

Children benefit psychologically from enlightened conversations about anger. With an absence of guilt and hostility, kids could have the scope to explore anger in its destructive and constructive incarnations. They would easily and naturally reorient themselves away from destructive anger because it is not pleasant to experience, and they would easily and naturally reorient themselves towards constructive anger because that is pleasant to experience. Rather than futile attempts at behaviour change through guilt, shame, or humiliation, I would like to change tact and try behaviour change through empowerment.

CHAPTER 12

You Are Your Psychology

I have formally been a student of psychology for more than ten years, initially as a literal student at university and then as a figurative student within my practice, seeing my clients as repositories for my own personal enlightenment—an endless array of case studies. I amassed anecdotal evidence from my clients day after day and year after year in pursuit of my own psychological mastery. I think I came to this life with a natural flair for psychology. I was the one at school who people spoke to because I was a good listener. I could empathise easily, and I would bring a balanced perspective.

I have never formally been a student of religion. I grew up with a grounding in Christianity, and it is certainly my mother tongue, but I regard myself as a lover of all things spiritual and it is that which runs through my veins. I believe the union of spirituality and psychology to be a powerful concoction. It has been for me at least, and these are my two great loves. The often esoteric nature of spirituality was grounded for me by psychology. My humanity could walk comfortably about the gardens of psychological constructs and psychological modalities while my divinity could soar about the clouds.

Because of these dual obsessions, I have found myself good at encapsulating the ineffable in simple yet psychologically resonant terms. It is my hope that you have found this to be true in your experience as you've read through these pages. I would like to take us on something of a detour now—or perhaps more precisely take the scenic route—in order to stoke the fires of your own empowerment. I know I have gone to great lengths to explain and espouse the psychological and spiritual mastery of your revolutionary child. But in order to offer any wise guidance to children, as I know parents are wont to do, you yourself should have sure footing about your own empowerment and a solid understanding of your own enlightenment.

It has been my experience in my clinical work that life is not so much "like a box of chocolates" as it is like a bucket of Legos. Stay with me here—this may initially seem off-topic, but there is a little bit of groundwork I'd like to lay before we launch into how you might become the empowered, innovative, awe-inspiring, pioneering parent your revolutionary child needs. René Descartes famously said "I think, therefore I am." Now I'm no Descartes expert, so with that disclaimer firmly in place, I'd like to suggest that Western philosophy might not have appreciated the spiritual profundity of Descartes's words as much as it has the intellectual profundity. Because of our Westernised love affair with reason and the intellect, much of his work was taken as a foundation for knowledge, whereas in my opinion, his words clearly portend an exquisite foundation for spirituality.

And here is where the Lego comes in. I believe that we can come to the essence of Descartes's work with a literal reading of his famous line. Peppered throughout his musings is the subtle, and at times not so subtle, truth that you *are* your thoughts, literally. At the basis of every great religious tradition, every great philosophy, all the great artistic movements, and all the great myths is the exploration of the human mind. At the basis of every great scientific tradition and every great medical advancement is the exploration of the human body. When these body and mind threads are woven together, the tapestry clearly shows a connection between physical existence (body) and non-physical existence (mind). We call this connection Spirit, and it is sublime but indefinable. No great surprise I know, alert the papers, "physical and non-physical still a cool mystery". If you can appreciate the nuance of the tapestry, you can reap psychological insights and spiritual revelations exponentially. Through the vehicle of psychology I believe spiritual revelations can be discovered and clarified in more concrete terms ... enter stage left: Lego..

Imagine every thought you have as a Lego piece. If we took this as literal truth, we could say that there two discernable properties inherent in a singular block of Lego:

1. It can belong to an infinite number of larger, more complex structures, just like thoughts.
2. By extension, it can be involved in construction or destruction, just like thoughts can.

Remember, in an earlier chapter, I was talking about how your attitude or your emotional tone about a party will impact upon your experience of the party? This is what I'm talking about here, but we are going a bit deeper with it. Legos can build stuff. Big stuff, small stuff, complex stuff, simple stuff. You can put two pieces together (construction) or you can take two pieces apart (destruction). Of course, there are other, obvious qualities to a single block of Lego, like colour, size, and shape, but we will focus on the two qualities above for the time being.

If we were to say that every thought is a block of Lego, you would have to agree that with your thoughts, you build your experience. If you think that a party will be terrible, you are building a mental expectation of displeasure. You are also conjuring an emotion of boredom or displeasure. So far so good. But what if we were to extend and deepen this idea and say that how you think about a party in your powerful Now literally creates your future party experience? To say "I think therefore I am" in Lego terms, we see that Descartes was articulating the notion "I think therefore I build," or "I am because I think," or "I built when I think." In this sense, you literally *are* your psychology.

The human mind is not really capable of non-thought; this is the essence of much of Descartes's work. While there may be short periods of non-thought—or more accurately, a slowing down of thought, usually by virtue of meditation—by and large it's unnatural for our minds to not think for long periods of time. If you can accept, at least for now, the premise that thought is literally an act of creation, then the idea that it's unnatural for us to not create because it's unnatural for us to not think will begin to make sense to you. Descartes was saying that while the mind can formulate many ideas and beliefs and opinions about many subjects, when you strip it all back to its most basic level, the mind just thinks. And this, he said, is evidence of supreme personhood.

I would like to say that while the mind thinks, the mind creates, the mind constructs. It can think about war, it can think about supermarket shopping, it can think about a garden, it can think about unicorns, it can think about knee surgery. But when you transcend the *what* of thought and find yourself in the *how*, you have entered the creative realm. Going further, when you have transcended questions about what your mind ponders and entered into contemplation about how your mind thinks, you are in the arena of Spirit. Irrespective of what your mind ponders, the fact that it quintessentially just thinks means that you are a creator at your very core.

Descartes was getting at this notion that the *what* can be disregarded because it is ever-changing. I can change my mind about anything if I want to. I can form an opinion and then form a different one. I can think something for no other reason than because it's what my mother thinks or my company thinks or my nation thinks. It is these thoughts that are the building blocks of reality, the constructor of personhood, of society, of humanity, of am-ness. Spiritually speaking, I believe Descartes' famous contemplation to be almost synonymous with the statement attributed to God when speaking to Moses, "I am that I am." Here the author was eloquently and poetically making reference to three spiritual Truths. It's like a three-note chord consisting of the eternal Now-ness of experience (one note) as well as, the duality of experience, (another note) and the constructive nature of thought (final note). Can you hear that harmony?

Let's take those notes in order, one by one, and I will see if I can play this music in a way you might be able to hear it—and then we can relate it back to empowered parenting and children. Firstly, the eternal Now-ness. The author's use of the word *am* coupled with *that* is deliberate, although it sounds like a grammatical error. The tense sounds mixed up linguistically because present tense is used on purpose to avoid any invocation of past tense. To say it simply, the author wanted to avoid the trap inherent in our common dialect of "God was" or "God did." It would have sounded more correct for the author to say something like "I was that" or "I am who," but such phrasing does not carry the same connotation of eternal Is-ness.

He is referencing and emphasising the eternal Now-ness of personhood. The author understood that Now is the only time that literally is because while you can reflect upon the past and you can predict the future, you are always doing it from your Now perspective. You are fabricating within your mind when you speak of past and future, not fabricating in the sense of deception but in the sense that past and future are mental events. Past events literally do not exist anymore within a three-dimensional, linear, space-time reality. Past events have gone, at least within this linear time, and Now these events do not exist, although they may endure within your mind. Similarly, future events, within linear time, literally do not exist yet. They may have some pseudo-reality in your mind, but any moment in time that sits outside of Now is a mental construct. When you arrive at a point in time that is five minutes into the future, that will be your new Now; when you were at the point in time called "five minutes ago," that was still your Now moment, when you were there. Applying words like *past* and *future* help conversationally, but in reality you are always in your Now moment.

The author wanted to capture the essence of this eternal Now-ness, and he could have equally expressed this as "I be who I be" or "I is that I is." As a human, you are always in a state of be-ing or is-ness or am-ness. Spiritually speaking, if you believe that an aspect of your personhood is eternal, you will always be in some form of be-ing-ness or is-ness-ing or am-ness-ing. As you can see, the conventions within our vernacular do not allow much scope to articulate spiritual Truths about eternity or is-ness. Hence the dilemma when putting such a concept into written word and the resulting, unusual wording when translated.

Let us take a second pass at it and I'll see if I can strike the second note (a major third above the first note, for those musical boffins playing along at home). I believe that the author was not just making reference to the eternal is-ness of all things but was also hinting towards the duality of the human experience. Both the Buddhist tradition and the Taoist tradition add to this glorious spiritual symphony of which Jesus was also part. The truths espoused by Jesus were equally spoken of by master orators like Lao Tzu and Buddha, but there have been many others besides. In many spiritual and religious texts, the use of capitalisation denotes an air of the sacred, a holy quality. To an extent, this is the best tool that we have in the written word to encapsulate the sacrosanct. If I took liberty with the author's statement and wrote it as, "I am that I Am," you can see how this simple phrase is hitting many notes all at once and creating sublime music. I believe that the phrase not only speaks to our eternal nature but can also speak to the duality of the human experience: "I am (humanity) that I Am (divinity)."

Thirdly and finally, at a perfect fifth above our first note, I believe that you can read the statement in a manner that beautifully and precisely harmonises with Descartes' work. Let me see if I can explain it sufficiently, and perhaps you'll hear the timpani's crescendo and the cymbals crashing. Try reading the statement in this way: "I am [pause] … *that* [emphasis] I am." In other words, "What I think I am … that *is* literally what I am," or "I am [fill in the blank] … that's what I am." I believe that Descartes particularly found resonance with this chord and added more notes to it in his own right. If you try to hear the tune being played, it is one of spiritual power and psychological power and creative power. I believe that Jesus and Descartes and Buddha and Lao Tzu and millions and millions of others across history have been talking about the creative power of thought, the creative power of your psychology, and the spiritual essence of your psychology.

Children come into life with this music still ringing in their ears, hence their psychological and spiritual mastery. If we, as parents, could recapture this song for ourselves, what a glorious world it would be. Descartes, his predecessors, and his contemporaries attempted to illuminate the enigmatic nature of mind and spirit, but they didn't have the benefit of my Lego metaphor, so this should hopefully make sense to you in a new way. Let me see if I can lay some of the groundwork now for the next chapter. I would like to offer a basis for understanding the nature of thought itself, because in order to successfully collaborate with your guru—your child—you will need to have some appreciation for children's spiritual and psychological prowess.

If each and every thought you have is a tiny piece of Lego, what type of Lego land are you constructing? Try to think about this in a literal way if you can. I often speak with my clients about the power of their thoughts, the power of their psychology, the power of their being-ness. Children remember this, but adults have forgotten it. The younger children are, the more clearly they recall. We adults, we are a forgetful bunch, and children do well to tolerate us.

I was talking to a client recently who has been struggling with chronic pain issues. During every session, I would try to help her find some relief—not from the physical pain she was experiencing but from the emotional suffering related to the physical pain. I explained to her that reducing or eliminating the suffering aspect would have an immediate positive impact upon her relationship to the pain. Her experience of the pain would be lessened because physical pain – emotional suffering = relief.

My client was an incredibly determined and passionate woman. She possessed a strong drive and an even stronger will. She was used to identifying problems and bringing her exceptional resilience and stamina to them. She was a tackler of problems; she could wrestle any issue. However, when the pain issues arose, she found herself caught in a bind. Under the current circumstances, she could not offer the type of action she was accustomed to. Her mobility and flexibility were significantly compromised. Her action approach was redundant now because she could not physically push through as she had done in the past. She had been forced to depart from the familiarity of her action-oriented world and venture into the unfamiliar territory of an emotional and spiritual world.

Understandably she felt completely lost and scared, and she was attempting to fall back onto her old, reliable, well-known coping strategies. She wanted an action plan from me; she wanted a to-do list. She desperately wanted to *do* something about her predicament.

She wanted to do the active things that used to bring her joy and confidence, and she wanted to achieve the same amount of housework that she used to. Her thoughts became increasingly fixed and rigid, much like her body. With each visit I made efforts to massage her thinking, but it was to no avail.

One of the biggest challenges I encountered with this strong-minded, strong-willed client was the *but*. I spoke passionately with her about how transformation was not just possible but inevitable, and I spoke with certainly about how she might embrace this difficulty and move through it with the talents already in her possession. I spoke with fervour about how powerful and influential she was and how a small change of mind, a slight adjustment in her mental trajectory, could yield wonderful results, but ... it's the darnedest thing. As sometimes happens, she continued to offer me some variation of "But ... it's so hard!"

People will say things like "But ... you don't understand," "But ... I just can't embrace positives in the midst of this challenge," "But ... you don't appreciate the complexity; my problem is bigger than that," or "But ... you just don't see, it's hard to stop thinking in negative terms when it's such a habit for me." I guaranteed my client that she'd jumped over a myriad of hurdles in her life. She had faced a multitude of challenges successfully. She had smashed through a host of obstacles victoriously. But she could not share my vision, and I just became an annoyance to her.

This client was a classic representation of somebody who did not appreciate the power of her own psychology and the creative power of her own thoughts. She intellectually understood that her thoughts were contributing to her emotional agony, but she saw her emotional journey as entirely separate and secondary to her action journey. I wanted her to prioritise feeling better, but she wanted to prioritise do-ing better.

I'll pause briefly here and ask you what type of parent you think you are. Are you an action-oriented parent? Do you want to throw down with your child's issues? Do you want to wrestle your child's problems into submission? Do you take your child's fire and sass and independence and free spirit and see them for the psychological mastery they are, or would you like your child to be more docile? Do you harbour a secret desire that your children will just do as they're told for once? I know I've certainly harboured this desire on more than one occasion, and it hasn't been such a secret, I'll assure you.

Ponder for me, if you will, what sort of relationship you've constructed with your child. Have you been approaching your parenting from an action perspective, or are you able to alter it slightly and make the emotional tone of your relationship paramount? Have you been trying to *do* the relationship into a better place, or could you allow for the possibility that thought and, by extension, emotion are the more powerful components in any Now moment? With this premise in mind, I hope it makes sense to you that it is thinking better and feeling better that actually contribute most strongly to positive situational change, *not* action.

I met with a loving and wise and oh so helpful mother recently who was very action-oriented. She was becoming increasingly troubled by her son, who had some sensory processing issues and was hanging out in anger a lot of the time. When he was in the throes of anger, she would offer suggestion after suggestion of what he might *do*. Her own intellect and resourcefulness had led her to acquire a lot of knowledge about what might be helpful for him. She would suggest a weighted vest, she would suggest his iPad, she would suggest a hug, she would suggest a small dark tent (which can be soothing for kids with sensory issues). With every suggestion, her son would grow more and more agitated and increasingly resistant.

When I asked this frazzled mother if she felt confident in her parenting, she offered a resounding *no*. She quickly qualified her statement by saying, "I try not to show him that I'm frustrated, but I am very frustrated." She went on to say that sometimes she became so overwhelmed by a desire to be helpful that it verged on desperation. When her efforts were thwarted by her son, she didn't know whether to scream or cry.

Just like my client with chronic pain, this mother felt that if she offered the appropriate action, like helpful suggestions or a reasonable plan or multiple options, her son would be comforted. But when you are parenting a child, especially a child who's on the autism spectrum or has sensory processing issues, you're dealing with a psychological master. This young man's sensitivity levels were so acute that he could sniff out his mother's frustration or despondence at a thousand paces. While she tried to feign confidence, he was easily able to call her bluff. He could attune to her emotionally, and it was throwing his own emotions off-kilter. This mother and son personified the internal conflict of my chronic pain client, who was trying to think her way through an emotional problem and was, in fact, inflaming the issue.

The Lego land that my pain client had constructed for herself was a hellish, depressing place of limitations and broken dreams. But because she wasn't literally picking up a physical piece of Lego with her physical hand, moving her physical muscles, and placing it upon another physical piece of Lego, she struggled to understand how her mind could hold such monumental creative power. Her physical eyes could not see the creations forming piece by piece, and without the physical evidence as a reference point, she was left to rely upon the emotional evidence. The fact that her creations were making her feel hopeless and miserable was obvious to her, but we were swimming out of her depth in these emotional waters, and she wanted the sand beneath her feet again. She wanted the sure footing of those physical banks.

Action, not emotion, was her forte. She grasped the emotional concept intellectually, understanding more so that her emotions were unpleasant and unwanted, but she could not extend that knowledge in order to fathom that it was her mind that constructed her land of Lego. She knew that her thoughts were unhelpful, and she appreciated that unpleasant thoughts would make her feel unpleasant—depressing thoughts are depression-making—but she did not extend this understanding to the fact that those unpleasant thoughts were very, very powerful. She could not understand that her thoughts were imbued with the power of Spirit, the power of God, the power of creation.

Let's rewind and use our imagination to envisage a time before my client was injured. Imagine her working in a confident and capable way. Imagine her happy in her marriage and joyful on her days off. Imagine her revelling in motherhood and loving her friendships.

All day, every day, quite unbeknownst to her, her thoughts were positive, by and large. Let's say positive thoughts are like colourful little Lego pieces. All day, every day, with each thought, she was unintentionally placing little pieces of Lego onto her creations (not physically, remember, but with the power of her mind, Matrix-style). On balance, the overall world she created was pleasing to her. She would relax in her lovely Lego house, walk the lovely Lego streets, get about in her lovely Lego car, and sit and chat with her lovely Lego friends.

Everything about this Lego utopia had been constructed inadvertently. She had created by default. She was not deliberate about her thoughts. She observed, for example, the house she had created and "saw that it was good." She was able to observe the marriage she had created and "saw that it was good." Imagine a life-size Lego house, imagine a full-size Lego husband and son. I know there are limitations to any metaphor, but just go with it for a while. Remember, I am not talking about what she had created on an action level; I'm asking you to imagine her psychology as the creative driver behind her life. She would think things into being. She may have quickly and unwittingly thought something like, "I'll help my son with that job"—a little, insignificant thought, you would presume. But imagine that such a small, solitary thought is like placing a dusty brown Lego piece onto a head of hair of a Lego avatar. This life-size Lego model is a perfect replica of her son, who stands with wide eyes and toothy grin in the corner.

The emotional set-point she held (her psychology) about her marriage or about her home or about her mothering was confident and capable, loving and helpful. The thoughts that she had amassed around these topics were innumerable and largely positive. While she would very rarely be mindful about her happy, confident thoughts, the outworking was evident by the manifestations. Her thoughts regarding her husband and son and work were positive overall, and this literally created a positive experience, thought by thought, one piece at a time. A heavenly Lego world. This is the esoteric meaning of "in the beginning was the word." Thought, extended into word, is the impetus behind all creation.

Now imagine the days immediately after her injury. If she had not encountered physical injury in her life before, thoughts about limited mobility or physical pain would be relatively novel within her mind. In the beginning, she might have given voice to optimistic thoughts like two brightly coloured Lego pieces locking together: "I cope okay with pain" and "I'll recover okay." Obviously the genesis of any creation is not this straightforward, but for the sake of simplicity, let's imagine what she might have constructed with these two thoughts. It's like two Lego pieces interlocking at right angles. It's nothing really. If your child brought you this creation, you would behold it with curiosity, wondering what it was supposed to be. At this stage, it is indeed no-thing.

My client's world remained largely intact. Her beloved creations still stood, and the emotional tone of her life was positive and optimistic, so pain was simply brought into the fold and thought about through this lens. The two rogue pieces were simply clutter upon the floor, easily disregarded and unproblematic. But then a year of chronic pain goes by. Doctor's appointments happen, surgery happens, physiotherapy happens, pain medications happen, and what was a nondescript creation in the corner has been added to over time. Pain thoughts have become more common, and medical thoughts are more familiar in her mind. The tone has shifted, and these pain thoughts are no longer positive and optimistic. They are pessimistic, negative thoughts. Many, many, more thoughts have contributed more and more pieces, and the pieces have become increasingly dark.

Thoughts about her family and her home and her friends may remain positive, but the pain thoughts are leaning towards pessimistic. The pain thoughts are tinged with hopelessness. While the foreboding pain creation seemed to be confined in the beginning, now the black and grey tones are encroaching upon other creations in her mind: *I can't see friends because of pain* (one piece). *I can't clean the house because of pain* (another piece). *I can't help my son because of pain* (another piece).

When you think about the situation from an action perspective, it is easy to see why people believe they have isolated a problem or controlled its ramifications. My action-oriented client paid no mind to her thought process because she was simply trying to act her way to recovery: *I've been to the doctors. I've spoken to the surgeon. I've done my rehabilitation. I take my medication.*

When you lack an understanding about the power of your thoughts, you can be left reeling from the confusion. *Why am I not getting better? I'm doing all the right things.* Just as with our earnest mother who was convinced that presenting her son with action alternatives would relieve his anger, while somebody may appear to be doing all the right things, it will not necessarily alter their being-ness.

On the one hand, my pain client was doing recovery in a formulaic, traditional way, and she had been led to believe that this was what healing was all about. She had initially found solace in the medical myth that prescribed actions will yield improvements, but years on she was no better and in fact was worse in some regards. She was having great difficulty reconciling the apparent contradiction between rote, medicalised action, and a worsening condition. This reconciliation was difficult because she did not put a lot of stock in her being-ness. She expected to act her way to wellness, to intellectualise her way to improvement, and yet she found her emotions to be unruly, overpowering, and unpleasant. She was be-ing pessimistic but do-ing the right things, she was be-ing resentful while do-ing what was medically advised, she was be-ing scared while trying to do confidence.

With these years of pessimistic thoughts and resentful thoughts and fearful thoughts, the Lego pieces of her old life came crumbling down. Not all at once, just one piece at a time, gradually and imperceptibly. It's like she would pass by her garden bed and think to herself: *I hate the garden now, it use to be so pretty. I can't even do my gardening anymore. I use to love gardening. Another thing I can't do.*

Being naïve about the power of her thoughts, she did not appreciate that she was essentially reaching down and plucking the little Lego flowers from the little Lego garden bed and breaking them apart in her hands. Her negative attention upon the garden was having a destructive effect within her mind. The next day, as she passed by, she would think: *Now that pretty yellow flower has died. I can't even bend down to pull the weeds. I couldn't even turn the soil with a trowel. I wish this garden bed wasn't even here. I hate looking at it.*

All of the little Lego flowers were gone, and now as she walked by her thoughts were creating weeds—dark Lego weeds. Imagine that each thought was represented by a single grey Lego piece. She would pluck five pieces from her pocket daily, connect them together, and place them atop a weed stem already standing there awaiting completion. Ironically, the next day she would walk past the garden bed on her way to the letter box, and she would make note of the ugliness of it within her own mind. But it was literally those thoughts of ugliness that were constructing the ugly weeds. Thinking depressing thoughts was creating a depressing experience.

When you don't appreciate the power of your own psychology, you can become like the crazy lady who is out in the garden muttering under her breath, "I hate these weeds. These weeds are so ugly. I wish I had some flowers. I really, really hate these weeds," all the while plucking the flowers from the garden and planting row upon row of weeds.

If you mustered enough courage and sidled up to the crazy garden lady, you might be tempted to say, "If you hate the weeds, why not plant some flowers or at least stop tending to the weeds?" But when you are naïve about the power of thoughts you are oblivious to the creative force behind them.

The crazy garden lady would snap, "Don't be stupid, I'm not tending to the weeds" (as she continued to lock a dozen more weedy-black Lego pieces into place). "This soil is cursed. Flowers just won't grow for me."

"Oooookayyyy," you'd reply as you backed away slowly, palms raised, avoiding eye contact.

For the majority of people, thoughts come at them like a barrage. We are inundated by information in this modern age, and the consequent impact upon our thoughts is that they come at us thick and fast. As soon as you awaken, your mind can easily launch into thoughts about the to-do list—your own, your partner's, your children's. As soon as you arise from your bed, you can plug into Facebook or Snapchat or Instagram or Twitter and find your thoughts hooked into world news or local scandals or a friend's gossip. You might check your e-mail and be drawn into the latest drama at work, and what's more, it apparently requires you immediate attention.

Whenever I saw my client, I'd ask her how she had been doing since our last session, and she'd proceed to bombard me with an account of the problems and the pain and the issues and the lack of solutions and the lack of improvement and ... and ... and. As fast as I would try to deconstruct the weeds and make some pretty Lego flowers in their place, she would come in behind and, with a sweep of her hand, knock down the pretty Lego flowers and build up the weeds again, up, up, up into the sky. As she thought her hopeless thoughts and then gave voice to them, she was oblivious to the hopeless reality she was constructing. She was reaping what she had sewed, and yet she felt indignant about the miserable crop.

The gloomy thoughts would fly through her mind like bullets sprayed from a machine gun. The pace was so fast that she stood little chance of discernment as they bombarded her. And this is the case for most adults. Thoughts flash through their mind at such lightning speed that they are surprised by their subsequent creations. They will tell me:

"I don't remember thinking negatively about my son's report card."

"I don't remember thinking pessimistically about my daughter's friendships."

"I don't remember thinking about my parenting style at all."

When I am speaking with clients and introducing them to the power of their thoughts, they will often be ten thoughts into a miserable story before I politely interrupt and point out that ten unhelpful thoughts just went flying past. Frequently clients will look at me bemused as if to say, "But I'm just telling you what the situation is." Adults think on the basis of accuracy; they think on the basis of truth and the current reality. Unless they coach themselves to do so, adults do *not* think on the basis of happiness or empowerment in the way their child counterparts do. Isn't that an interesting thing? It is a by-product of adult intelligence that we prioritise truth and accuracy over happiness within our own minds.

Disempowered or anxious or depressed thoughts are an indication of your current reality—this is true. It was obvious why my client was thinking about the discomfort and inconvenience of her pain. Her pain *was* uncomfortable and inconvenient. Simple. But it's like poison in the river upstream. If you knew there was a toxic plant spewing noxious chemicals into the river system, you would be unlikely to drink the water that flowed to you downstream. You would at least mistrust its safety, and rightly so. You would wander up to that pesky chemical plant, stem the flow of poison in whatever way you could, and then as the river slowly cleared and cleaned, and cleared and cleaned there would be fresh, life-giving water to drink.

When I would speak with my client who was struggling with chronic pain, she would declare:

"I am in chronic pain."

"I have been in pain for a long time."

"I don't know how I will stop being in pain."

All of these statements were true and accurate given her current circumstances, but equally they were depressing and disempowering, regardless of her current circumstances. They were like poison in her emotional stream. These thoughts were tainting her emotional experience and turning it sour. When I suggested that we use a different criteria for her thoughts, she would argue for her current process—and by extension, she would argue for her current limitations.

"My thoughts about these things are true," she would announce. "This is what's going on. I'm not making it up." Thinking so as to feel happier was a bizarre concept for her to get on board with. It just sounded crazy to her, and I knew it, but I was relentless in my desire for her emotional improvement. It would, after all, be no less accurate for her to say: "Yes, I've got a lot of pain, but I am hopeful about ..." "Yes, I've got a lot of pain, but I do find relief in ..." "Yes, I've got a lot of pain, but I'm optimistic because ..."

"See if you can reach for a slightly happier thought for the sheer fact that you want to feel happier," I implored. But by this stage, my client had convinced herself that I misunderstood her situation. In essence, I was beseeching her to not drink so readily from the river with the pungent, dirty water. What a sad indictment on adults that we cling so tightly to accuracy and sensibility, to the realistic and the factual, that we seldom allow ourselves the luxury of a story embellished with positive outcomes and positive expectations. If you are stuck in a depressing reality or a painful reality or a fearful reality, then accuracy is not your friend.

Now, I'm not suggesting you stick a yellow smiley-face sticker over problems to make them go away. But when you are aware of the power of your psychology, you begin to be slightly more selective about the account you give, the words you choose, and the Lego land you are creating. In deference to our spiritual and psychological masters, it is clear that a thought process peppered with lying, denial, overconfidence, imagination, selfishness, or ease is psychologically healthier and spiritually more aligned—not just because it's nicer to think happy thoughts, not just because it feels better to feel better, but because when you harness the power of your psychology, your happier, nicer, better-feeling thoughts will literally shape your reality for the better.

CHAPTER 13

Empowered Parenting: Do It Your Way!

I was speaking with the mother I mentioned in the last chapter together with her husband. This extremely loving mother was incredibly well informed regarding the psychological and sensorial and medical and educational strategies that could potentially assist her "angry" son. In stark contrast, her husband sat beside her quite even-tempered and nonchalant.

At our initial meeting, I asked, as I always do, for a nutshell description of the problem. This big-hearted and eager mother launched into a monologue about the plight of her son. She had obviously been through this process with other professionals before. She give a breakdown of symptomology, antecedents, historical factors, triggering events, precipitating factors—we covered it all, and with fancy lingo to boot. She explained to me that their son had a good school year last year. Prior to that, he had been attending a different school, and the semester was nothing short of terrible. Their son was the target of bullies, and this spurred aggression in their young sage. His teacher had been unsympathetic and would often scuttle his desk outside of the classroom where he would sit alone in mock solitary confinement. This year their son's teacher was ostensibly "okay" but too laissez-faire for their rule-bound son.

As I sat and listened patiently, this very intelligent and beautifully loving mother's psychoanalysis of her son got me thinking. Many parents I encounter are healers by nature, but they are frustrated healers at best and wounded healers at worst. They are frustrated because they have stayed overlong in union with their proverbial patient. Many psychologically minded, insightful parents have studied the wound-ology of their child and invariably they have made an accurate diagnosis. Their child *is* often stuck in anger. Their teenager *is* probably trying drugs, and that may not turn out so well. Their daughter *should* speak more kindly to them. What's more, these psychologically astute parents have prescribed the appropriate balm. If only he were more calm ... if she would just apologise ... if his friends were the sporty type ... they would not have these problems.

The trouble with human beings is that pesky free will thing. Children hold staunchly to their freedom, tweens and teens even more so. Your beloved child can sit politely in your personal consultation room and listen to your wise counsel about the perils of drugs or the particulars of good manners or the benefits of negotiation. But he or she is free to walk out of a consultation with you carrying a concoction of loving advice and not take the medication as prescribed. There is no inherent Truth that says kids "should" take your well-meaning advice. They will not apply generously after bathing, they will not take 2 hours after each meal. In fact they are completely free to throw your pill of loving advice in the gutter the second they leave your presence.

This is the real meaning behind the verse, "Physician heal thyself." Being entangled with loved ones while secretly harbouring an agenda to rescue or enlighten or change or heal them is an act of judgement on your part, albeit subtle and packaged in a pretty box. When you imagine somebody to be in need of rescue or healing or fixing, you are not seeing that individual's splendid essence. You are paradoxically inhibiting your ability to be an effective healer because you have broken your own divine Hippocratic oath. First, do no harm!

This mother was very sincere in her desire to help her son. But her attention to his wounds made her feel like he was in need of rescue and healing. She had been journeying down from her own mountain peak to meet him in the swamplands of anger and hopelessness. He did not appreciate her efforts, and he made it known. In the midst of his angry outburst, she would fly into problem-solving mode and try to hug him and soothe him and fix him. It's like she would clamber down into the bog and wrestle him to the ground in order to tie a rope around his waist. She would then attempt to haul him up while he kicked and thrashed and savagely gnawed on the ropes with his teeth, screaming, "Leave me alone, I want to do this myself!"

Every futile effort on this sweet mother's part was draining her of optimism, energy, and clarity. When you notice that your child is in the throes of anger or sadness or fear, that is not the time to try to coach him or her into calm deliberation. Many parents I speak with lament that "When I ask him what's wrong, he can't tell me." Of course not! It's much more difficult to stem the flood once the banks have burst.

Imagine your child's thoughts are like a rip. Your thoughts are just like this too if you'll notice, but for the sake of the metaphor let's think about it from your child's perspective. Once anger or sadness or anxiety has taken hold to a chronic degree, it's like a rip has developed in their mental ocean. If the child goes swimming in the vicinity of sadness, they can get pulled by the rip into depression—not because of poor willpower, not because of a sinister and diabolical problem, not because the child is bad, but simply because these are the physics of thought. If you go swimming in the vicinity of judgement and condemnation, a rip may pull you into anger or resentment. If you go swimming in the vicinity of worry, a rip may pull you out into an ocean of anxiety. Once a rip has a hold of you, there is such a strong pull it's futile to fight against it.

As adults, we often encounter individuals who have been pulled into anger. In the common vernacular, we say that somebody "snapped" or "saw red." We are also well aware when people are being pulled down into an ocean of sadness; we say they are "drowning" or "suffocating." Within the psychology of these individuals, there is strong momentum that is pulling in the direction of depression. While they would love to swim out of it, they become fatigued by the effort.

Sometimes very well-meaning parents will try to coach their children to swim against this emotional current. If kids are angry, for example, parents may try to rationalise them out of it by saying, "It's not as bad as you think," "You're just not thinking logically," or "You need to calm down." But you don't fight an emotional current directly. You don't swim *against* it, you swim *away* from it. It is like parents are standing on the beach screaming at a drowning child, "Just swim harder, swim this way, swim harder, swim harder, this way, this way!"

In Australia, we are all very familiar with the physics of a rip, but at some of our most popular beaches, where many tourists descend, there are frequent, near-fatal drownings when unsuspecting swimmers are caught in one. They panic and become easily disoriented because it seems so logical to swim against the rip towards the beach. The shore is in sight, and making a beeline for the shore seems like the most sensible decision. And yet, beneath the waves, there is an unseen force working against their efforts. To say swim *away* from the beach seems crazy to a drowning individual, because it appears to be going in the wrong direction.

When children, our psychological and spiritual visionaries, employ emotional strategies like ignoring or distraction or changing the subject or anchoring into fantasy (editing the story to suit themselves by, for example, lying), they are attempting to swim away from the problem into calmer emotional waters. When you give your kids the benefit of the doubt and comprehend that they are not enjoying being churned around in the waves of anger any more than you are, you can be more like their lifeguard than another hapless victim. Coach them to swim away, *not* against. Better still, just stay out of the water and allow them to swim away themselves. They will naturally do it if you'll let them.

In the middle of an oceanic current, your psychological sage will naturally reach for whatever slight improvement they can find. If you come along just as your child is reaching for the lifebuoy and try to initiate a conversation before he or she is ready, you might as well be snatching the buoy from your child's grasp and holding your child's head under the water.

Imagine your child is swimming away from a strong current. For a little while, it may seem like he or she is not really getting anywhere; there is still some drag. A slight improvement on angry thoughts may be overwhelmed thoughts: "This feels too big for me" may be a slight improvement on "I hate your guts!" So may "I'm not even talking to you" and "I'm leaving." Stay out of the water and understand that your child will instinctively do as Dory does: just keep swimming, swimming, swimming. Once your child is headed into the clearer waters of hopefulness—*that sucked but it seems better now*—he or she will quickly come into the vicinity of indifference. Now your child is a few strokes away from contentment, and then the shores of happy are within reach. So elegant, so natural, so instinctive ... if you can trust the process.

As much as you can, wait until your child is back on shore before you attempt to help him or her with any negative emotions. Our kind-hearted mother didn't notice the rip that got a hold of her son and dragged him out into the terrifying depths of anger. She misunderstood her role in the whole ordeal also. In the midst of the problem, as she talked about it and focused upon it and fussed over it, she was essentially withholding the life preserver. She had swum into the uncharted waters of her son's ocean (uncharted by *her*, not uncharted by him—or more accurately, his Spirit), and she'd become snagged too.

To exhaust this little analogy, it was Dad who was relatively serene and unflappable. He surfed up confidently on his jet ski heroically asking, "Does anybody need help here?" He commented that their son was much less oppositional with him, and it was immediately obvious why. This father was confident. This father was an empowered rescuer.

There is a perfect irony to relationships—a glorious, stupendous, transcendent, perfect irony, and you'll love it, I promise. First, you must let people be different from you. I know this sounds simple and hardly in need of pointing out, but many understand this tenet on an intellectual level, not an emotional one. In reality, you don't have any choice but to let people, every person, even your children, be who they choose to be, because people will be who God is calls them to be and not who you call them to be. Your children will be who they were born to be. This may be somebody you find easy to get along with or somebody you find difficult to get along with. But we are all expanding and evolving creatures. By that I mean that we are all gathering lessons along our life's path, and we are all coming to our own personal realisations and our own individual revelations and our own private inspirations constantly—children especially.

If you encounter your child in a powerful Now moment carrying the assumption that he or she will be exactly the same as yesterday or last week or one hour ago, then you place limitations on both of you. Your intellect tells you that "people don't change," and your intellect tells you that continuity is likely: "My child will probably be the same today as yesterday." But you limit other people by presuming that they cannot, or have not, grown, matured, and expanded. You limit yourself because you carry the baggage of history into what could have been a new, fresh, and vibrant beginning. Let people be who they need to be. Be humble enough to appreciate that you might not be the authority on who somebody is.

You may not bear witness to the best version of your child. Indeed, you may see your children at their worst. When you've had a ringside seat at another person's circus, it is incredibly easy to presume that you know the acts; after all, you've been watching the show up close and personal for such a long, long time. But be humble; just try to be humble. Allow for the possibility that there are other acts back there behind the curtain, acts that you've never seen, acts that you didn't even know were there.

I have often sat and talked to adult daughters who tell me that their mother was uncaring, their mother was too critical, their mother was spiteful or judgmental. I have often sat and spoken with mothers who say that their daughter was uncaring, their daughter was too critical, their daughter was spiteful and judgmental. Who is right? Is it me or is it you? Is it us or is it them? Don't be a lazy thinker as a parent. If you have come into conflict with your child, felt frustration or concern, and seen things that you dislike or judge, then you have lost sight of who your child really is. You are not beholding your child through the eyes of Spirit. Your intellect might insist that you know more about other people when you have borne witness to their personal brand of crazy for year after year after year, but in fact, the exact opposite is true. Unless you seek to love and accept others just as they are, you can never truly understand their essence.

"Seek ye first the kingdom of God ... and all else will be added unto you" means to first seek to love. Often what we think of as love or what we call love is actually highly conditional, particularly when it comes to parental relationships. We might profess to love the other, but it's a kind of subtle ruse, a profound misunderstanding of what love actually means. Love is a verb; it is a doing word. When you say you love your child but have lost sight of his or her glorious essence, its like you have handed your child a beautifully hand-wrapped gift embellished with ribbons and bejewelled with precious stones. "I love you," you say. But upon unwrapping, a swarm of wasps flies out and stings the recipient to high heaven.

If you've ever notice yourself saying, or thinking things like "I will accept you a lot easier when ...," "Yeah, I could be nicer to you if ...," "Sure, I could be more loving, but ...," then you have delivered a beautiful-looking parcel to your child or tween or teen which, upon unwrapping, will leave him or her reaching for the calamine lotion. If you first seek to love and surrender to the Truth of who your children are—that is, utter perfection, because their essence is perfect, their Spirit is perfect—then you can recognise that their personality is an imperfect expression of this perfect essence. First seek to love this imperfect expression.

Now, the way children express their essence isn't always pretty. The way they express their essence isn't always easy to take. It isn't even something you need to stick around for at any given moment in time. But if you first seek to love, an amazing thing happens. When you are practicing acceptance and confidence and calm, you are finally in an empowered position. Now you have something to offer somebody: your empowerment!

This is what my client's father was embodying. He felt much less concern about the well-being of his son. He stood with more confidence in his own parenting abilities. He carried less self-doubt. He was lighter about the whole ordeal. He was trying to do less, and therefore was able to be more. He was like an alchemist in the epic, grand mythos of his family. The magnificence of an alchemist is their ability to transform base metals into gold. Within any challenging or concerning relationship, parents have the profound ability to perform a little alchemy. Mothers and fathers who have discovered how to be masterful wizards or powerful witches can take a child's intention to offend, or a teenager's pointed insensitivity, or a tween's outright bitterness, and elicit and invoke the gold.

Confidence is the first, prerequisite ingredient. With that, you can wave a magic wand over fear and *abracadabra* it into love. A pouty "You never let me do anything that I want!" from a teenager is poured into the beakers and boiled over the flames and becomes "I think what you are trying to say is that you want what you want, and that's okay. I often want what I want too. I can understand your frustration." In the absence of this magic, in the absence of grace and wisdom and confidence, parents are wont to say, "Well I'm just trying to help you" or "Do it yourself then, you ungrateful cow." However, a seething "I hate you, you're such a bitch!" when sprinkled with magic dust hocus-pocuses into "I know you're angry, and that's fine, but I'm going to leave you with that right now."

Is it an art form? Absolutely! Does it take deliberate effort and practice? Certainly! Is it an indication of your exquisite power? Hell yeah! There is a good reason why the alchemist was revered, and empowered parenting is the ultimate elixir.

When you approach parenting in a formulaic manner, in a socially acceptable manner, often it is other parents who are appeased. The topic of parenting is fraught with know-it-alls and two-cents givers. Those in the peanut gallery offer their unsolicited advice and biased agendas. I guarantee, unless you are talking to a spiritual master or a psychological oracle, you probably don't want to put too much weight into other people's opinions about your child. Yet many adults search for their confidence and self-esteem amongst the spectators. If a grandparent or a friend or an expert or a fellow parent agrees and approves of your parenting decisions, that feels so much better than being out on a limb by yourself.

For me personally, I underwent some seismic psychological changes in my own life about eighteen months ago, and it was a very empowering and enlightening process. It was my out-on-a limb experience. It was like I was huddled around the trunk of a tree with all the other people from my community, all of my family members and friends. We stood on our respective branches bunched up safe and secure. As I underwent this transformation in my own spiritual life, I deliberately moved away from traditional dogma and dove into universal, gnostic spirituality. It was a liberating, exuberant time, but I was taking one step out on my branch.

Members of my family and members of my traditional church community stood resolutely at the trunk. Some would perhaps risk extending a hand, as their other arm firmly grasped the trunk, but they could not understand how dexterous I was becoming. I could balance; I was sure-footed. They worried for me out there. They offered sentiments like "It's dangerous out there" and "You'd better be careful." What to me felt like a thrilling tightrope walk to them seemed like peril.

Over time, I gained confidence being one step out on my limb. Then came the next step. I arrived at a personal decision about divorce, and I decided that I was going to end my marriage. This was like another huge step out on that limb. There were fewer people around me now. In the eyes of gawkers, I was getting weird, I was becoming strange—culturally speaking, anyway. Again, I encountered many of my own psychological barriers, including hurdles about the idea of marriage, divorce, and about the idea of family and what that entailed. I came face to face with the judgment and condemnation of society at large. But I was on a roll, and I was unperturbed. I was balancing with the agility of a mountain goat now, and while I left behind many at the trunk, I was not about to sacrifice my growing empowerment for anybody. Balancing my way back to the security of the trunk would have felt like stagnation, like devolution.

As I settled into my niche two paces out on my limb, I encountered another of my own psychological barriers. I was being called way, way out as issues of sexuality came to the fore. Another step out on my limb, and even fewer people were prepared to join me. The entire process felt like a psychological stripping back. As my dependence and reliance upon other people's approval waned, my personal empowerment grew. I anchored firmly into self, and few others were bold enough to make the journey out there with me. The experience taught me that being guided by other people's opinions will hold you in the comfortable bosom of the tribe but does not serve personal empowerment. It is not the path of the revolutionary. Individuals can only know for themselves whether they are closer to or are further away from Source.

Some children may be coming most spectacularly and deliciously into their power when they watch exotic videos on YouTube, but if you are suspicious of exotic YouTube videos, you might lay down the old, "Oh, why would you want to do that?" Some teenagers may be coming awesomely and powerfully into themselves within a new relationship—you just happen to hate the new partner. You might pull out the old, "Oh, are you sure about this one?" But you can never judge what is authentic and empowering for another person. Empowerment isn't a spectator sport; you need to suit up and get out onto the field yourself. So keep your eye on your own parenting game and play for all you're worth.

When we try to parent based upon broad, sweeping social customs, we often guide children and parents alike down a generic and oversimplified path. We debate and squabble in order to reach some kind of consensus about good parenting. In so doing, we can lose the subtlety and nuance of the whole ball and dice. As each individual is unique unto the universe, each relationship is equally unique. There is no right way to parent any given child, and there is no right strategy for every parent. There are broad psychological strokes and general spiritual guidelines, but at some point parents must be empowered to trust their own instincts and follow their own inner guidance.

The action-oriented mother I have been describing throughout this chapter asked the perfect question as we arrived at this juncture in our conversation: "So should I just do what my husband does then?" The last pieces of her action-oriented approach were whittled away, and she was still thinking in terms of do-ing.

"No" I said. "Do not seek to *do* what another parent does, even when it's the father of your own child. You will bring your own unique, authentic, empowered style to parenting unlike any other." A parent who believes that she must *do* parenting in the "right" way is straightjacketed when it comes to her own creativity and confidence and inspiration. A parent who believes she is do-ing something wrong in child-rearing is a disempowered parent indeed, a mere shadow of her true Self.

If we adhere too staunchly to the conventional parenting milieu, we are in danger of perpetuating social norms about right and wrong and good and bad. Progress, evolution, and awakening are slow going under these conditions. Mothers may hold very accurate ideas about self-love and self-care, while fathers may hold very accurate ideas about confidence and calm, but you can only teach what you are, not what you know. When mothers are brimming over with resentment and fatigue, they will teach low self-worth and self-sacrifice by their example. Any lip service to the contrary is wasted breath. When fathers are pent up with frustration and hopelessness, they will teach aggression and emotional detachment. Given the psychological and spiritual nous of kids, they will invariably "do as you do, not as you say."

Conventional wisdom suggests that we should teach our kids to control and contain their emotions. Sounds good in theory, doesn't it? Anger is considered particularly unseemly. We tell tweens not to yell, we tell toddlers to be quiet, and we tell teenagers not to grab or stomp or throw. While obviously these are valuable lesson for kids to learn over time, and there are obvious non-negotiables about nonviolence, it is often the case that adults in the lives of unruly or distraught kids are, themselves, noisy when angry or irrational when upset. Isn't it interesting that, as adults, we know the nature of anger to be loud and abrupt, sometimes stubborn, sometimes illogical, sometimes hurtful? We know the nature of concern or worry to be irrational, sometimes powerfully so. Yet we ask kids to do anger or worry or sadness in the most unnatural of ways. If you, as an adult, don't always know how to contain anger and yelling happens, why are kids held to often impossible standards? If you, as a parent, find yourself drowning in worry or caught in sadness and crying happens or withdrawal happens, why would it be different for kids?

Now, don't misunderstand me. There is a difference between constructive anger and destructive anger, chronic sadness and transient sadness. But rather than putting a blanket ban on emotions altogether—which is impossible because they're a necessary part of the human experience, especially for children—we could be at peace with all emotions and bring them into the fold as a feeling to be expressed, not suppressed. I envisaged my client's father as a noble, majestic lion. He was king of his pride, and he knew it. When the young lion pounced on his back looking for a tussle, this father was obliging ... to a point. He was not afraid to assert his role as the alpha male, but he effected this role with quiet confidence. His meekness belied his strength.

I asked this father how he "did" anger, and unsurprisingly he confessed that he could raise his voice at times and he could say things that were not well thought out, but there was little aggression in his anger. Some fathers mistake bravado for confidence. Some fathers mistake macho for masculine. There is a fine line between assertive and aggressive, and often fully grown men have not learnt how to tame their emotions and channel them constructively

CHAPTER 14

When Mum Is Trying to Be Dad and Dad Ends Up Resembling Mum

In modern times, we have lost some of the magnificence of the masculine. The sacred warrior has morphed into the wounded warrior, and the divine father has transmuted into the absentee father. Foolishly, women will often try to assume the role of both the feminine and the masculine in the lives of their children. This may be for many and varied reasons, all of them perfectly justifiable and reasonable. Women may argue that their husbands work too much or that their partner won't step up. Men may complain that their wives are too controlling or too critical. When parents come upon an impasse in their parenting, usually there are accusations flying around along the lines of:

"You're too soft with them."

"Well, you're too harsh on them."

"You let them get away with too much."

"Well, you don't let them have any fun."

"He needs to learn to follow rules."

"He's just a little boy."

The sacred balance of yin and yang, masculine and feminine, mother and father is lost when a father criticises a mother for her feminine attributes—her gentleness, compassion, and patience—and a mother disparages a father for his masculine traits—his assertiveness, confidence, and directness. While these dynamics may seem to hold true only within heterosexual relationships, they can also be seen within homosexual relationships. It isn't about the sex of two parents or a matter of male and female so much as the gender roles that are naturally assumed by the two.

Broadly speaking, masculine qualities are of the intellect and physicality. Resourcefulness and resilience, sensibility and capability, rationalisation and intellectualisation are born of the masculine. When the pendulum swings too far, an extreme masculine presents as macho, mentally rigid, overly intellectual, stubborn, and aggressive. It's the classic king archetype in malevolent form. For this masculine archetype, the scales have tipped, and feminine qualities have been muted. Broadly speaking, feminine qualities are emotional and spiritual in nature. Intuition and mysticism, compassion and kindness, patience and wisdom are born of the feminine. When the scales tip, the extreme feminine presents as emotionally unstable, lacking in emotional boundaries and emotional resilience. It's the classic damsel in distress archetype—a bleeding heart and a submissive nature. In its extreme incarnation, this feminine archetype has lost balance, and masculine strengths are subdued.

The harmony of masculine and feminine can be lost within an individual, intrapersonally, as well as being lost within a relationship, interpersonally. Fathers may try to ally with their young sons to guide them through boyhood into manhood, but all too often fathers feel emasculated by their wives. Historically, women have enjoyed the benefits of feminism and social movements directed towards the empowerment of the feminine. While the pros and cons of this issue could provide enough fodder for a book in itself, suffice to say here that feminine characteristics are somewhat more esteemed, at least in theory. Yet paradoxically, they are not, as yet, well enacted or embodied by men or by women.

Men are considered effeminate when they walk or speak in a certain manner; they are deemed "metrosexual" when they dress or look a certain way. Meanwhile, we have reduced the sacred feminine to a look or a posture. This is like asking a child to describe an exquisite crème brûlée and the gross, simplified description "it's custard" is considered satisfactory. In truth, a man who has mastered the feminine is not "female." Personifying the goddess has little to do with dress or speech or gait. A man who can embody the feminine is deeply compassionate, wonderfully patient, superbly intuitive, and sexy as hell! He is no less masculine; in fact, his masculine nature is enhanced, not diminished.

In our modern age, women have forgotten their queenly nature. As men play in the sandpit of the feminine, women have ostensibly left it altogether and are raiding the masculine sandpit, throwing sand in the boys' eyes and telling them, "Get out, I wanna play here." Women are naively playing at masculine and believing it to be some kind of "new feminine." In truth, a women who has mastered the feminine is still a confident, strong leader, but she leads as a matriarch. She is not trying to fit into patriarchal notions of power and strength. A woman who owns her femininity is a priestess. She is mysterious and seductive and elusive and wise. But she is certainly not lacking in power or influence.

So while the notion of feminine is being redefined culturally by both men and women, I would say that our revisions are still in their draft form. Our notions of masculinity are undergoing a revision also, but that is still in its fledgling stage. Men are groping around in the cultural darkness trying to be good fathers and good husbands. Within a strictly patriarchal society, the masculine is entrenched, esteemed, and pervasive. In this context, the role of the father and husband is clearly defined, albeit one-dimensional. In our modern culture, we are leaving behind strictly patriarchal ideologies and moving into greater balance. However, we are not as far down this road of balance as we'd like to imagine. In the ensuing confusion, all bets are off, and men are often left feeling guilt for the sins of their fathers, as it were.

Men don't want to be macho, but they also don't want to be effeminate. With the tectonic plates of society shifting beneath our feet, women are also floundering and attempting to be both mother and father. They are struggling in their efforts to be dad and mum, leader and lover, provider and princess. As women are increasingly embroiled in masculine arenas, particularly at work, they are called to organise, negotiate, problem-solve, formulate, strategise, and intellectualise. This mindset is carried over, often unconsciously, into home life as the family is organised and scheduled, problem-solved and negotiated. Amid all this gender confusion, dads often feel redundant. Men who feel like their role has been usurped by extremely capable, incredibly resourceful, highly intelligent women can be left struggling to find their place.

Under these circumstances, disengagement by fathers is certainly understandable, if not desirable. Alternatively, men will sometimes become Mr. Mum, retreating into the feminine realm. They may surrender to their fate as the submissive dolt, as the yes-man. Or they may emotionally vacillate between anger and depression. In their anger, they may have a short fuse or be very irritable. In their depression, men will often turn to alcohol or pornography or solitude.

We—and by that I mostly mean women—have overthought, overanalysed, and overly contrived the masculine so much that men feel they are more like castrated dogs than majestic lions, they are more like Maasai Warriors with aprons. So why are we surprised when a generation of young men and women feel psychologically lost and confused? We have mothers who behave like harsh judges or sappy nursemaids raising sons to be emotionally fragile (disempowered feminine) and daughters to be arrogant (disempowered masculine). We have fathers who behave like cruel kings or spineless servants raising sons to be naïve about their masculinity (disempowered masculine) and daughters who lack self-worth (disempowered feminine) And the results? We have a generation of tweens and teens who are enacting the extremes of gender norms. Young boys are either macho and arrogant or infantile and dependent. Young girls are either conceited and passive-aggressive or sad and powerless. Nobody is really happy in the process. It may seem like a big, huge, hopeless mess, but what have we learned about psychological and spiritual mastery? When confronted with hopelessness and powerlessness, children and adults alike will reach for anger first.

It is the fiercely independent masculine in a young man that causes him to rebel. Indeed, it is this fiercely independent masculine in a young woman that causes her to rebel too. And some young women certainly seem to be learning how to claw and scratch and growl with the best of them. A young man isn't a man without his own opinions; a young woman isn't an Amazonian warrior without her passion. A young man isn't a prince without his strength; a young woman isn't a priestess without her confidence. If we could let young men and young women be who *they* decide to be first and foremost, their emotional turmoil would be soothed. You wouldn't need to worry about the manifestations of disempowerment.

I could write you a long and varied list of the many faces of disempowerment. Well ... I sort of did really, didn't I ..., just up there ..., a few sentences back. Trust me, I really know what I'm talking about when I describe the psychological nuance of disempowerment. It comes from a decade of up-close-and-personal professional study. The dynamics, as I've described them, are accurate, I guarantee it. The dynamics, as I've described them, are valid.

Disempowerment is disempowerment is disempowerment. If we lump it all into a basket and call it all unwanted, we can turn our attention to what is important: empowerment and enlightenment. If you, as the parent to a sanguine child, could just provide some relief, if you could just soothe the situation, you can become a catalyst for change. If you can reflect first upon your own level of empowerment and make that your primary goal, then just like the father I've described to you throughout this chapter, you will be more confident, you will be more inspired, and you will be more relaxed. And aren't you an awesome parent when you're confident and inspired and relaxed? Don't answer that, let me tell you: emphatically yes!

CHAPTER 15

Inspired (In-Spirit) Parenting

You help an angry child by being calm. You help an anxious child by being confident. You help a sad child by being happy. Try not to "do" confidence and calmness and happiness. Embody those things, and you will find yourself more inspired about the doing part.

Can you be inspired in the action you offer about parenting? What is an inspired thought anyway? The word *inspired* comes from a root word meaning "in-spirit." Think about what it is like to receive inspiration about something. Maybe you were inspired to call somebody and that person was just thinking about you too. Perhaps you were inspired to design something and it set in motion a chain of events that culminated in making something for a wedding or a birthday. You were inspired to stop for coffee and it led to meeting a business acquaintance which led to making a new friend which led to meeting your new partner. We easily overlook seemingly banal thoughts and, most interestingly, the perfunctory nature of such thoughts can makes you think it's just you thinking.

What if you are receiving constant spiritual guidance? What if Source-God-Love is literally dropping thoughts into your mind all day, every day, but you don't recognise common place thoughts as in-spirit thoughts because, in the privacy of your own mind, they sound so much like you? What if the line between you and You (body and soul, humanity and divinity) is like a gossamer thread, a silk veil, barely perceptible?

I was speaking with a long-term client last year. She has two tween daughters, and both were worrying her for different reasons. Her youngest daughter was of particular concern because she refused to sleep in her own bedroom. My client was cut of the cloth of the divine mother. She was extremely graceful, and when she spoke it was like the tweeting of a canary. She was also incredibly sensitive and intuitive, as if she might break into song at any moment while birds landed upon her outstretched palm and deer frolicked about her shins.

This mother had recently started a new relationship, and her partner was equally sensitive and intuitive but less delicate and graceful. As this very loving, gentle mother was inclined towards lenient, laissez-faire parenting, her partner was inclined towards the "firm but fair" approach. For many, many months, this mother sought my help regarding her own troubles, but we occasionally touched upon her parenting dilemmas. Together we explored the pitfalls and the potentials of a punitive approach. We also explored the pros and cons of laissez-faire parenting. We surveyed the parenting landscape, and we mused about the relative advantages and disadvantages for her daughters.

After several conversations, I had my own moment of inspired thought. I sensed very powerfully that, intellectually, this mother understood why solid boundaries and natural consequences and firm guidance are all good things in their right measure. This mother also deeply understood that compassionate guidance and empathetic negotiation and emotional wellbeing were also good things when kept in balance. She intellectually understood it all, and I quite literally mean *it all*. And yet something was amiss. When I had my epiphany, I realised that it was her confidence that was missing. This delightfully instinctive, sensitive mother was not trusting her own instincts.

I asked her to disregard everybody else's opinion, ignore what her partner wanted her to do, pay no mind to what her daughter might think, ignore the parenting books, discount everything that I had said, and forget what her friends and her sister thought. What did *she* want to do? And you know what? She knew. In her own Spirit, she just wanted to leave the situation be. In her heart, she wanted to let it play itself out. When she left the consultation room that day, she was changed for the better because we had made great strides towards restoring her confidence.

If your head is in the driver's seat when it comes to parenting, you are more inclined to try to do confidence. Your intellect will think about what confidence should sound like and what confidence probably looks like. But confidence is not a state of doing, it is a state of being. When you try to do confidence in an inauthentic way, children know it.

Take the action-oriented mother we discussed earlier and her confident husband. When I made it clear to this loving mother that she would do well to restore her confidence, she took it as an intellectual challenge rather than an emotional one. Her intellect jumped into action, and she thought, *So I should just do what my husband does.* Her intellect then went on to spin a tangled, convoluted web: *But I can't do what he does. I don't know how to do what he does. But perhaps I should do what he does. He thinks I should so what he does.* Her intellect had taken the problem by the horns. If your head becomes power hungry and insists upon being in control and reducing everything to a formula to be solved, your heart (emotion/Spirit) is relegated to the passenger seat, riding shotgun. Your heart is not allowed to take the wheel.

I was speaking with a client recently who was having great difficulties at work. This client was much like the gentle mother I have described to you, only this client was even more dainty and temperate. Think the voice of Marilyn Monroe with the air of Audrey Hepburn. In her workplace, it was unsurprising that this soft-spoken women had been designated tasks that did not technically fall within her jurisdiction. This longstanding dynamic had resulted in her feeling overworked and underappreciated.

Despite her self-sacrificing nature, the management at her workplace had recognised her innate wisdom and would often promote her into temporary leadership roles. This was equally unsurprising to me, because the foundation of this woman's self-sacrificing nature was also the foundation of her leadership capabilities. She was kind, extremely kind. But her kindness could flip on her and become a shadow aspect of her personality.

Natural kindness can easily manifest as selflessness, particularly within our culture. When this woman was able to channel it constructively, it was the driving force behind her diplomacy, her excellent work ethic, her collaborative abilities, and her compassionate nature. Put simply, it made her an exceptional leader. Despite this, when she was honoured with leadership positions, she was riddled with self-doubt. She would receive compliments about her talent as a leader, and she would immediately undermine this flattery within her own mind.

Intellectually, she knew she was doing a satisfactory job because intellectually she knew, probably better than anybody there, what was logistically required to do the job well. But it did not matter what anybody else said regarding her work performance. In her estimation, it was subpar. Her intellect was ruling the roost, and it was a cruel taskmaster. Management and colleagues would appeal to her heart in the hope that she might *feel* more confident, but their compliments always fell flat.

Her intellect was not just undermining her confidence. Her intellect was not just keeping her heart from revelling in confident feelings. Her intellect had convinced her that doing a good job meant overextending herself, picking up slack from co-workers, arriving early and finishing late, and sacrificing her time and energy. According to her intellect, confidence amounted to little more than martyrdom. Her intellect had conjured an *idea* of confidence that was socially accepted but not truly empowered. She had become overly reliant upon her thoughts, and her heart was deep in protest.

When her intellect was trusted to make an approximation of confidence, it walked like sacrifice, it talked like sacrifice, it looked like sacrifice, because it was sacrifice! Her intellect was throwing around decrees like:

"We should do that job for him."

"They will be angry if we don't finish this off."

"I'd better go at their pace even if the result is sloppy."

"Just keep them happy. Just do it their way."

All the while, her heart was saying, "Let me drive, oh please, please, let me drive. I know how to be confident, I know, I know."

Confidence is heart work; bravery is heart work; courage is heart work. The more her head held fast in the driver's seat and refused to relinquish the wheel, the more her heart made its protest. And how did it protest? She began to feel stressed, she began to feel depressed, and she began to feel anxious.

Here is something you may not yet be aware of: anxiety is not the enemy it has been made out to be. Neither is anger, and neither is sadness. What if every part of you was your friend, but you have just fostered a relationship with anxiety that is mistaken? My client certainly came to me believing that something was going seriously wrong. She was sure that she shouldn't be feeling stressed, and she was sure that her growing resentment was a problem to be done away with. But just like you can form an erroneous assumption about a person—she is shy, not rude; he is confident, not arrogant—anxiety or stress or anger can be seen as wrong and bad and a problem when in fact they are blessings.

In my client's predicament, if her intellect was left to its own devices, if it was allowed to navigate the journey, my sweet client would still be working overtime. She would still be doing the work of three people. She would still be exhausted at the end of her day, with no energy for her family. Stress and anger and sadness are indeed your friends, because they can certainly shake you out of complacency and rationalisations and justifications. To say it differently, your emotions can insist upon having your attention. Emotions are a clearer channel for spiritual guidance. Source can get your attention with a generous helping of stress.

There is so much static on the line when it comes to the intellect. As I've said, my client was merrily tripping along thinking that sacrifice was actually good leadership. Once her heart wrenched the wheel from the grasp of her head and veered them off into the woods, the trajectory had changed and Spirit had its invitation. As your friend, emotions have something important to impart. Your emotions carry their own wisdom. My client's heart was calling her through stress; it was calling her through anxiety.

When did anxiety visit with her? At times when she felt the most limited. Anxiety visited when she felt self-consciousness or self-doubt. Anxiety visited when she found herself most vulnerable. So what if stress was not her enemy telling her to "suck it up, princess"? What if anxiety was not a monster telling her to be perfect and not say anything stupid? What if anger was not a shadow telling her, "You're so pathetic!"? Then her emotions were her friends. And your heart is your friend also.

I know that there are times when you think you are not doing a good enough job as a parent. I know there are times when you second-guess your decisions or feel the burden of raising a happy, successful human being. I know it's really tough, and you'd just like to know it's all gonna be okay. Please let me assure you that it is all gonna be ok. Don't take my word for it, take your own *feel* for it. Redirect yourself back to your own wisdom.

Your negative emotions are telling you, "This limiting belief doesn't serve us anymore, my love, let's let it go."

If fear is your friend, she is telling you, "I think we have a chance to be really brave here. Let's go for it! Awesome sauce! Trust your gut, even though it's scary as hell"

If self-doubt is your friend, she's telling you, "This belief makes us feel like crap. Let's dump it, sweetheart!"

We erroneously tell ourselves that if we just let our heart guide us, we'll be pushovers, our kids will run amok, we'll screw up our kids and they'll hate us forever more. Our intellect is so accustomed to sitting in the driver's seat it truly believes that, if your heart were to take the wheel, it will get you irrevocably lost. My client faced this precise dilemma. She thought that if she gave herself permission to go with what she felt—namely, "I want to feel more relaxed because I feel stressed and bitter"—then she would be a bad employee.

It took tremendous strength for my client to give herself permission to ease off at work. Her intellect was freaking out like an overprotective parent offering misguided thoughts like *What will happen? ... You can't do this! ... What will people think? ... They won't like you anymore! ... Something terrible might happen!* Your head is suspicious of the navigational skills of your heart, and your head is convinced that if you allow your emotions to drive, you will veer off the road to an inevitable crash. But while your head (intellect) can lead you on a merry jaunt in its efforts to navigate the way to Happy-Ville or Confidence Town, ultimately it does not know how to get there.

My client drew upon her resources of insight and courage and wisdom and decided to follow her heart. She so desperately wanted to feel better that she made ease and happiness her primary goals. She turned the whole situation around in a matter of a week. Was it intimidating for her? Absolutely! Did it need to get to that point before she prioritised her own happiness? No, but all of us need to walk our own path in our own way. Was it an empowering experience? You bet your ass! Your emotional (spiritual) wisdom is so powerful and instinctive that, as *A Course in Miracles* tells us, your "slightest willingness" is all that's necessary for Spirit to inundate the circumstance and restore love and balance and wisdom. Clarity and confidence flood into the situation and trump any thoughts to the contrary.

As we sat and debriefed about the whole experience, I emphasised to my client that she now had a visceral experience of confidence. Previously she might have thought she was being helpful, but now she understood that helping others at her own expense was helping nobody. Previously she might have thought that it was selfish to leave other people's work to other people, but now she understood that if she didn't have the time or energy to help, it was kind to allow others their own empowering experience. As she learned self-care and self-confidence, they learned initiative and responsibility.

So how about you? Do you lead with your heart or with your head? The distinction is artificial, of course; it is never a clear-cut case of either/or. But you might have noticed a tendency within yourself. Have you struck a good balance within your parenting between thoughts and emotions? When your head is in the driver's seat, you may find yourself deep in thought about what might make somebody else happy, but has it ever worked when you've tried to implement your plan? When your head is in the driver's seat, you may find yourself thinking about what will make somebody less angry, but has that ever worked when you've tried to roll out your strategies?

Oh, your head (intellect) will assure you that it knows the way. "Trust me," it says. You feel sure that if the other person just listened to your plan, just did what you suggested, everything would be great. You trust that your intellect can guide you to a happy resolution. Your intellect isn't above using manipulative tricks to secure its place in the driver's seat, either. It will convince you that the other person is the one who is screwing up the plan, it will deceive you into believing that it is the other person who needs to change. "Finding Happy-Ville is easy," says your head. "It's just beyond the next rise, it's just around the next turn. And finding Confidence Town is a piece of cake. I'm sure I've been there before. We'll just head west, I think that's right ... if that person would just get out of my way and stop veering into my lane."

But how long have you been driving around aimlessly relying overmuch on your intellect? What have all those good ideas amounted to? Temporary fixes maybe; frayed nerves certainly. Despite reassurances from your intellect, all that happens is that you end up lost in the dark forest of Frustration, or you end up at the dead end of Despair. And it's nobody else's fault.

Allow your heart to wrench the wheel from intellect's white-knuckled grip. Trust that it can lead you to your destination. Your heart may even want to drive through that deep forest of Frustration or on the rickety winding road of Worry, but your heart does not get lost in this challenging terrain the way your intellect does. Your intellect will end up in Worry City and declare, "We are lost!" Your intellect believes that negative emotions are so fundamentally wrong that any detour into worry or frustration or sadness is bad, and it will declare the whole journey a failure. In contrast, your emotions navigate by the North Star of your Spirit, and that is constant and sure and true.

Your heart doesn't worry about rocky terrain because your heart knows you are courageous. Your heart isn't perturbed by winding paths because it knows you are wise. Your heart isn't concerned about rivers to cross because it knows you to be creative. Even if you don't yet believe these things about yourself, your Spirit holds to this knowing unwaveringly. That's why Spirit is not concerned about leading you through difficult emotions.

Be more at ease when it comes to your magnanimous children. Chillax more. God has got it. Source has their back. They have angels at their side. Feel your way to ease. Feel yourself into relief. Your children are destined for greatness, and this is, in large part, because they have decided to elect *you* as their soul partner. A precious sapphire is smoothed by rubbing it against another precious sapphire. Own your position as the precious gem in their life. Don't seek to make their life easier, and don't seek to make their life harder either. Just drive joyously alongside each other, each person staying in his or her own lane as much as possible.

Remove your attention from your children's anger as much as you can, because your attention upon their anger makes *you* angry or sad. Trust who they really are. Trust that you know who they really are, even when they don't. Trust that you know who they really are, even when they are demonstrating the exact opposite. Just look into your child's eyes. Have a fleeting conversation over the breakfast cereal. Hold her hand or ruffle his hair. Let these be sacred experiences. Every mind is a temple, every conversation is scripture, every touch is love. *Mi Amore!*

ABOUT THE AUTHOR

 Deidre Steadman, BA, BHSc (hons), MPsych (clinical), is a clinical psychologist who has practiced in South Australia for the past ten years. Deidre has had extensive and diverse clinical experience working in the private sector as well as for government departments. Deidre is currently practicing as a clinical psychologist at Alpha Psychology, a private practice she established in 2012. She is a full member of the Australian Psychological Society and participates in the Transpersonal Psychology interest group.

Deidre is passionate about pioneering psychology into a new era. In addition to revising traditional psychological diagnoses and traditional psychological ideologies, Deidre is on the leading edge of psychological thought as she innovates psychology into the digital age. She lives in South Australia with her three young children: Oscar, Jasper, and Bethany.

You can visit the author and view her online psychological services at www.alpha-psychology.com. You can also follow Deidre on social media via Facebook and Twitter, or visit her YouTube site for free video content.

Printed in the United States
By Bookmasters